DREAM APARTMENTS
APPARTEMENTS DE RÊVE
TRAUMWOHNUNGEN

DREAM APARTMENTS
APPARTEMENTS DE RÊVE
TRAUMWOHNUNGEN

EVERGREEN

EVERGREEN is an imprint of

Taschen GmbH

© 2005 TASCHEN GmbH

Hohenzollernring 53, D-50672 Köln

www.taschen.com

Editor Editrice Redakteur:
Simone Schleifer

Editorial assistance Assistante d'édition Veriagsassistentin:
Marta Serrats

English translation Traduction anglaise Englische Übersetzung:
Richard Lewis Rees, Matthew Connell, Matthew Clarke (Introduction)

French translation Traduction française Französische Übersetzung:
Marion Westerhoff

German translation Traduction allemande Deutsche Übersetzung:
Susanne Engler

Proof reading Relecture Korrektur lesen:
Matthew Clarke, Marie-Pierre Santamarina

Art director Direction artistique Art Direktor:
Mireia Casanovas Soley

Graphic design and layout Mise en page et maquette Graphische Gestaltung und Layout:
Diego González, Jonatan Roura

Printed by Imprimé part Gedruckt durch:
Artes Gráficas Toledo, Spain

ISBN: 3-8228-4184-6

Contents Index Inhalt

The apartment is the logical evolution of the home in today's heavily populated world. Restrictions on urban space have obliged people to opt for dimensions that are more limited than those of a traditional house if they are to continue enjoying the advantages of living in a city center. The term "apartment", however, need not be synonymous with lack of comfort or unattractiveness – in fact, the aim of this book is precisely to demonstrate that the most functional small home can also be a magnificent example of innovative and evocative architecture.

Although apartments are becoming an increasingly popular choice for a new home, it is important to bear in mind that the design of a dream apartment is not necessarily simpler or cheaper than that of a family house. Limitations on space force architects to follow two premises: the need for integrated, versatile spaces and the preeminence of functional solutions (although these may vary according to the type of family setup for which the residence is intended). Although there is a strong tendency to flood settings with light, the first priority should be to organize the available floor space along lines that ensure the principle of habitability, even while breaking with traditional approaches to construction – after all, it must not be forgotten that the ultimate aim is not just to admire the resulting architecture but also to live in it!

Dream apartments is aimed at readers who resist the idea of homogenization sometimes associated with an urban apartment. The creative genius of the world's best architects has been put at the service of simple spaces enclosed between four walls that are not so very different in principle from many other apartments in our cities. No elaborate exterior structure can distract the critical eye from the work undertaken in these interiors: the designer, like us, starts from the same point – an empty space – and, through the skilful and ingenious use of construction skills, this can result in apartments as exclusive and inspirational as the ones presented in this book.

L'appartement est l'évolution logique de l'habitat dans un monde surpeuplé tel que le nôtre. L'espace urbain incite les citadins à opter pour un espace aux dimensions plus limitées que celles d'une maison traditionnelle afin d'habiter au cœur de la ville et de profiter des avantages qui en découlent. Ceci étant, le terme d'appartement n'est pas nécessairement synonyme de manque de place ou d'attrait. L'objectif de ce livre est donc bien de démontrer que l'habitat très fonctionnel peut être également un magnifique exemple d'architecture audacieuse et suggestive.

A l'heure actuelle, les appartements ont de plus en plus le vent en poupe auprès de la clientèle en quête de logement, mais ne nous y trompons pas : la conception d'un appartement de rêve n'est pas nécessairement plus simple ou plus économique que celle d'une maison individuelle. La limitation de l'espace astreint l'architecte, dès la conception, à tenir compte de deux impératifs : intégrer obligatoirement des espaces polyvalents et rechercher des solutions fonctionnelles optimales, modulables en fonction du type de famille qui habitera les lieux. De toute évidence, il y a actuellement un engouement croissant pour les espaces diaphanes. Ceci étant, il est recommandé d'organiser l'espace disponible autour d'une distribution des sphères de vie, assurément moins classique, mais sans sacrifier pour autant le principe d'habitabilité. Car pour finir, n'oublions pas que l'objectif ultime du projet n'est pas uniquement d'en admirer la réussite architecturale, mais de pouvoir y vivre.

Appartements de rêve est un livre destiné aux lecteurs qui se défendent d'associer la notion d'uniformité au concept d'appartement urbain. Le génie créateur des meilleurs architectes du monde s'est mis au service d'espaces simples, compris entre quatre murs, et qui en principe ne sont pas bien différents d'autres appartements de nos villes. Aucune structure extérieure tape-à-l'œil ne pourra détourner le regard du travail d'agencement réalisé à l'intérieur : le concepteur et nous-mêmes, suivons la même finalité, à savoir, métamorphoser quelques mètres cubes vides, à coups d'originalité et d'ingéniosité architecturales, en appartements exclusifs et innovateurs, à l'image des exemples exposés dans cet ouvrage.

Das Appartement ist die logische Weiterentwicklung des Wohnraumes in der heutigen, überbevölkerten Welt. Der in den Städten begrenzt vorhandene Platz hat die Menschen dazu gebracht, in Räumlichkeiten zu leben, die kleiner als das traditionelle Haus sind, um die Vorteile genießen zu können, die das Leben im Zentrum der Stadt bietet. Dennoch muss ein Appartement nicht gleichbedeutend mit fehlendem Komfort und einer weniger schönen Wohnumgebung sein. Ziel dieses Bandes ist es zu zeigen, dass auch eine sehr funktionell gestaltete Wohnung gleichzeitig ein wundervolles Beispiel für eine bahnbrechende und anregende Architektur sein kann.

Auch wenn es der heutige Trend ist, dass sich immer mehr Menschen für ein Appartement entscheiden, sollte man sich nicht täuschen lassen denn, die Gestaltung einer Traumwohnung muss nicht unbedingt einfacher oder billiger sein als die eines Einfamilienhauses. Aufgrund der räumlichen Begrenzungen muss der Architekt auf der Grundlage von zwei Voraussetzungen arbeiten. Einerseits ist es notwendig, die Räume zu integrieren und vielseitig zu machen, und andererseits müssen sehr funktionelle Lösungen geboten werden, die sich je nach der Art von Familie oder Einzelperson, die die Wohnung beziehen wird, ändern. Obwohl ein deutlicher Trend zu transparenten, weit wirkenden Räumen besteht, ist es empfehlenswert, die zur Verfügung stehende Fläche auf eine Art zu organisieren, die von den traditionellen Schemata abweicht, ohne deshalb die Bewohnbarkeit znopfern. Schließlich ist doch das letzte Ziel nicht die Bewunderung der architektonischen Lösungen, sondern das Leben und Wohnen.

Traumwohnungen richtet sich an die Leser, die sich dieser Idee der Vereinheitlichung, die oft mit dem Konzept Appartement in der Stadt verbunden ist, widersetzen. Die Kreativität der besten Architekten der Welt wurde in einfachen Räumen zwischen vier Wänden eingesetzt, die sich im Prinzip nur wenig von vielen anderen Stadtwohnungen unterscheiden. Keine beeindruckende äußere Struktur kann von einer kritischen Analyse der Arbeit ablenken, die im Inneren vollbracht wurde. Der Innenarchitekt und wir selbst gehen vom gleichen Ausgangspunkt aus, nämlich von einigen leeren Quadratmetern, aus denen man mit ein paar einfallsreichen und einzigartigen konstruktiven Eingriffen so wundervolle und einzigartige Wohnumgebungen geschaffen hat, wie sie in diesem Buch vorgestellt werden.

Shanghai, China

Jindi Cartoon Coolpix

The architects commissioned to renovate this apartment focused their intervention on an interplay of black and white, to bring out the spatial depth of the project. The owners had a very clear concept of what they wanted: precision. Rather than opting for a space that would be white throughout, they opted instead for color scheme abunding in contrasts – to remarkable effect. Though the living room and dining room share a single, central space, different areas are delimited by black 'frames' on the ceiling that define the perimeter of each separate zone. Decorative elements such as the rug in the living room add to what the architects dubbed the 'zebra effect'. From the living room, one can make out the laminated stainless steel structure that supports the dining room table, which also contributes to the contrast of transparency versus opacity. The abundance of soft, natural light ensures that all these elements are combined harmoniously.

Les architectes sont intervenus essentiellement sur les dimensions de la structure de cet habitat particulier en jouant sur l'association du blanc et du noir pour accentuer la profondeur spatiale du projet. Les propriétaires partageaient une idée concrète : la précision. Au lieu d'opter pour un espace totalement blanc, ils se sont décidés pour un contraste chromatique donnant un résultat unique. Le salon et la salle à manger partagent le même espace central. Toutefois, les univers sont délimités par les marques noires du toit, définissant le périmètre occupé par chaque zone. De nombreux éléments décoratifs, à l'instar du tapis du salon, accentuent cet effet « zèbre », ainsi défini par les architectes. Depuis le salon, le regard est attiré par la structure en lames d'acier inoxydable qui soutient la table de la salle à manger, simulacre novateur qui sublime le contraste entre transparence et opacité. La lumière naturelle assure l'union entre les éléments.

Die Architekten nahmen die große Struktur dieses ganz besonderen Hauses zum Ausgangspunkt, um durch eine Kombination von Schwarz und Weiß die räumliche Tiefe zu unterstreichen. Die Eigentümer wussten, was sie wollten, sie wünschten sich Genauigkeit. Anstatt eines völlig weißen Raumes wurde ein Farbkontrast gesucht, der zu einem sensationellen Ergebnis führte. Das Wohnzimmer und das Esszimmer befinden sich im gleichen zentralen Raum, die Bereiche sind jedoch durch die schwarzen Rahmen der Decke begrenzt, die jeden Bereich definieren. Zahlreiche Dekorationselemente wie der Teppich im Wohnzimmer verstärken diesen Zebra-Effekt, wie ihn die Architekten nennen. Vom Salon aus kann man die Struktur aus gewalztem Edelstahl erahnen, die den Esstisch hält und erneut diesen Gegensatz zwischen durchsichtig und undurchsichtig betont. Das Tageslicht verbindet die verschiedenen Elemente.

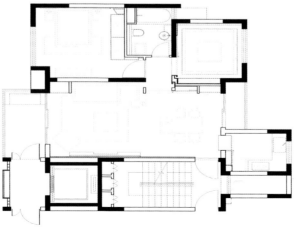

› Plan Plan Grundriss

The bedroom is really a prolongation of the central space, and reiterates the contrasting theme of black and white.

La chambre à coucher est le prolongement de l'aire centrale où là encore, le contraste entre le blanc et le noir est récurrent.

Das Schlafzimmer ist eine Verlängerung des zentralen Bereichs, wo aufs Neue der Kontrast zwischen Weiß und Schwarz zu finden ist.

The bathroom, adjacent to the bedroom, adds to this contrasting effect; on one of the walls, the owners have hung a distorted zebra-pattern print.

La salle de bains, attenante à la chambre à coucher, rehausse cet effet de contraste : un cadre est suspendu à un mur, reproduisant un poster de zèbre disproportionné.

Das an das Schlafzimmer angrenzende Bad unterstreicht diesen Kontrast. An einer der Wände hängt ein Bild mit einem verzerrten Zebramuster.

Ling Loft
Loft Ling
Loft Ling

New York, USA

The three-story 19th-century building that contains this loft was initially a factory for dental prostheses. The renovation started from the idea of creating an environment in which the clients could both work and live, while allowing the designers to experiment with a variety of materials, lighting elements, and spatial conditions. The division of the house into three zones - office, residence, and meeting space - is accentuated by the verticality of the sunken areas in which they are contained. These spaces were achieved by eliminating part of the structure between the lower floor and the basement, and by creating an intermediate level inside the overall volume. By doing so, the industrial character of the building was emphasized while also creating an interior reminiscent of a theater. In contrast with the original rustic materials, the office and meeting space were designed as metallic islands that would literally be surrounded by water.

L'édifice de trois étages, datant de la fin du XIXe siècle, qui accueille ce loft, abritait, autrefois, une usine de produits dentaires. La réhabilitation vise en premier lieu à créer un environnement réunissant lieu de vie et bureau et qui permette d'expérimenter divers matériaux, conditions d'espaces et d'éclairage. Les différentes zones -bureau, habitation et aire de réunions- sont définies par la verticalité des fosses qui les accueillent. Ces espaces ont été réalisés en éliminant une partie des fondations entre le rez-de-chaussée et le sous-sol et en créant un entresol à l'intérieur du volume général. Par ce procédé, les caractéristiques industrielles de l'édifice ont pu être exploitées au maximum tout en créant un espace intérieur très théâtral. Contrastant avec les matériaux rustiques d'origine, à l'instar de la brique et des poutres en bois, le bureau et la zone de réunions ont été conçus comme des îlots métalliques littéralement entourés d'eau.

In dem dreistöckigen Gebäude vom Ende des 19. Jh. war einst eine Fabrik für Zahnprodukte untergebracht. Durch den Umbau wünschte man eine Umgebung zu schaffen, in der man leben und arbeiten kann. Dazu wurde mit verschiedenen Materialien, räumlichen Bedingungen und der Beleuchtung experimentiert. Die Fläche wurde in drei Zonen Büro, Wohnung und einem Bereich für Zusammentreffen unterteilt. Diese Räume wurden durch Entfernen von Teilen des Mauerwerks zwischen dem Erdgeschoss und dem Keller geschaffen, so dass ein Zwischengeschoss entstand. So wurden die Besonderheit und die Materialien dieses Industriegebäudes hervorgehoben und es entstand ein sehr dramatisch wirkender Innenraum. Als Gegensatz zu den rustikalen Originalmaterialien wie Ziegelstein und Holzbalken wurden das Büro und der Bereich für Zusammenkünfte als eine Art metallische Insel, umgeben von Wasser, gestaltet.

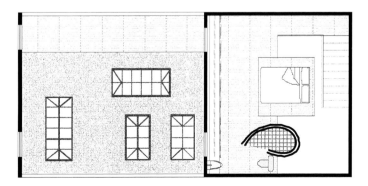

› Mezzanine Mezzanine Mezzanine

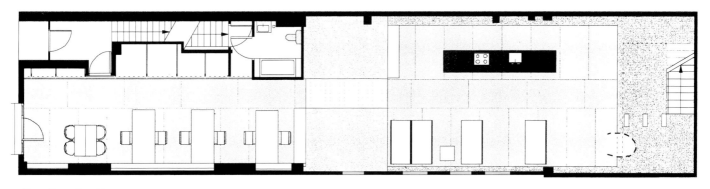

› Plan Plan Grundriss

Loftcube

Berlin, Germany

Loftcube represents one of the most brazen and alluring proposals to come out of Berlin's first-ever DesignMai design festival. Located on the rooftop of what was once a cold storage facility, on the banks of the River Spree, this building was transformed to reflect the paradigm of the nomad city - which requires a more mobile dwelling unit. According to the architects, we must rethink the architecture that exists around us, and rooftops in particular represent underused urban surfaces that may be re-marketed as sunny oases in urban areas. In their design, they took into account issues such as transportation, and the installation of handrails and services so that installing and arranging these volumes would be feasible. The idea is for tenants to be free to choose the colors, materials, and surfaces that best suit their tastes and needs, and even to adjust how much light enters the interior.

Loftcube est un des paris les plus audacieux et intéressant du premier festival de design Design Mai de Berlin. Installé sur la terrasse d'un ancien entrepôt frigorifique, à proximité de la rivière Spree à Berlin, il devient le paradigme d'une cité nomade qui choisit une unité d'habitat mobile. Les architectes ont souligné la nécessité d'analyser l'espace architectural déjà érigé pour mettre en valeur les terrasses comme étant des superficies urbaines délaissées, utilisables et commercialisables, car elles constituent des oasis solitaires dans les zones urbaines. Ils ont étudié les questions de transport, d'installation de mains courantes et de fournitures de matériel pour que l'installation des volumes soit possible. Le locataire est libre de choisir la couleur, le matériel et les surfaces au gré de ses goûts et besoins. Il est également possible de varier l'intensité de la lumière qui pénètre à l'intérieur.

Loftcube ist einer der gewagtesten und interessantesten Vorschläge zum ersten Designfestival DesignMai in Berlin. Das Loft befindet sich auf der Dachterrasse eines alten Kühlhauses in der Nähe der Spree in Berlin. Es hat Modellcharakter für eine Weltstadt voller Stadtnomaden, in der man auf eine bewegliche Wohneinheit setzt. Die Architekten vertraten die Ansicht, dass die bereits existierenden Gebäude analysiert werden müssen, um zu entscheiden, ob die Dachterrassen ungenutzte städtische Flächen sind, die als eine Art sonnige Oase inmitten der Stadt benutzt und vermarktet werden können. Sie berücksichtigten Fragen wie den Transport, die Anbringung von Geländern und die Lieferungen, damit das Aufstellen der Elemente durchführbar sei. Der Bewohner selbst kann die Farbe, das Material und die Oberflächen auswählen, die seinem Geschmack und seinen Ansprüchen entsprechen. Sogar die Stärke des Tageslichtes, das einfällt, kann reguliert werden.

The designers chose materials from DuPont, such as Corian, Zodiaq, and Antron, and mobile furniture systems, such as Case and Cube, designed by Interlübke.

Les matériaux choisis sont le corian, le zodiaq et l'antron de Du Pont et les systèmes de rangement sont des meubles portables, à l'instar du duo Case et Cube, signés Interlübke.

Es wurden Materialien wie Corian, Zodiaq und Antron von DuPont gewählt, und Systeme für tragbare Möbel wie die von Case und Cube, die von Interlübke entworfen wurden.

The 430 sq. foot interior is designed to allow one to live and work in an environment that can be adapted to one's tastes and needs.

L'intérieur, de 40 m² environ, est conçu pour vivre et travailler dans un environnement modulable au gré des goûts et des besoins du locataire.

Der ungefähr 40 m² große Innenraum ist so angelegt, dass er an den Geschmack und die Ansprüche des Bewohners angepasst werden kann.

Shanghai, China

Jindi Cartoon Coolpix II

The owners of this dwelling sought a space that could be experienced with all five senses. To this end, instead of creating a segmented surface, the designers opted for distributing the various areas in a single indoor volume in which arches in the ceiling indicate the use of each zone. In the center, a small, protected area - similar to a tearoom - subdivides the living room by means of two sliding glass doors. One of the aims of the design of this recurring space was to create a new way of interpreting the traditional use of tatami mats. The sliding doors allow the space to be left open while still maintaining the privacy needed to relax in a comfortable setting. The lively colors of some of the details mix with the pure, sober materials used on the floor and the walls. A series of lights built into the ceiling round out the lighting scheme in the interior.

Les propriétaires de cette habitation ont recherché un espace qui puisse interpeller les cinq sens. A cette fin, au lieu de créer une superficie sectionnée, le choix s'est porté sur la distribution des sphères dans un volume intérieur unique où les arcs du toit indiquent la fonction de chaque zone. Au centre, une petite zone protégée, à l'instar d'un salon de thé, subdivise la salle de séjour grâce à deux portes coulissantes en verre. La conception d'une nouvelle interprétation de l'habitat traditionnel autour du tatami est une des idées du design de cet espace récurrent. Les portes coulissantes permettent de garder l'espace ouvert tout en préservant l'intimité nécessaire à la création d'une ambiance détendue et confortable. La vivacité des couleurs de certains détails se mêle à la pureté et sobriété des matériaux employés sur le sol et les murs. Des plafonniers encastrés permettent de compléter l'éclairage intérieur.

Die Besitzer dieses Hauses wünschten sich einen Raum, den man mit den fünf Sinnen wahrnehmen kann. Dazu wurde anstelle einer in Zimmer unterteilten Fläche ein einziger Raum geschaffen, in dem Bögen an der Decke die einzelnen Bereiche voneinander abgrenzen. Im Zentrum befindet sich eine kleine, geschützte Zone, eine Art Teeraum, die das Wohnzimmer mit zwei verglasten Schiebetüren unterteilt. Bei der Gestaltung dieser Wohnung sollte vor allem das traditionelle Benutzungskonzept des Tatami neu interpretiert werden. Durch die Schiebetüren kann man den Raum offen lassen, aber gleichzeitig für die notwendige Privatsphäre sorgen, um sich zu entspannen und wohl zu fühlen. Die lebhaften Farben einzelner Elemente mischen sich mit der Reinheit und Schlichtheit der Materialien, die für Boden und Wände benutzt wurden. In der Decke eingesetzte Lichtquellen vervollständigen die Beleuchtung.

The arch in the dining-room's false ceiling articulates the various zones in the central space.

L'arc formé par le faux plafond de la salle à manger distribue les différentes sphères de l'espace central.

Der Bogen der abgehängten Decke im Speisezimmer unterteilt den zentralen Raum in verschiedene Bereiche.

› Plan Plan Grundriss

The television can be seen from any point in the house, as it rotates 180 degrees.

Grâce à un système de rotation à 180°, il est possible de voir la télévision de n'importe quel endroit de l'habitation.

Man kann von jedem Ort in der Wohnung aus den Fernseher sehen, der bis zu 180 Grad gedreht werden kann.

Garage/Living Room
Salon garage
Wohnzimmer Garage

São Paulo, Brazil

Architect and designer Brunete Fraccaroli's revolutionary concept with respect to architecture is that houses should be used in their entirety, and that living rooms should not be roped off and reserved for special occasions. In order to break this mold, she designed a living room that is contained entirely within a garage. Some of the surfaces are crafted in colored, interlaminated plastic, and others in transparent laminated glass, allowing the natural setting to permeate into the home. This project is a stunning example of how to give physical form to an attitude and lifestyle through architecture. Two spaces that are traditionally separated - in this case, the living room and garage - here live together comfortably in an intermediate atmosphere. Instead of reducing their functionality, the interaction between the two has been heightened. Additionally, the use of transparent glass ensures that nature can influence the indoor environment.

La conception révolutionnaire de Brunete Fraccaroli développe l'idée qui préconise l'utilisation de la maison dans sa totalité et d'ouvrir les salons à tous les visiteurs. Selon son concept de rompre les barrières, il a conçu un salon compris dans un garage. Pour certaines surfaces, il a utilisé du contreplaqué coloré, et pour d'autres du verre laminé transparent qui permet d'intégrer la nature à l'habitation. Le projet est un magnifique exemple de savoir-faire architectural visant à concrétiser une attitude et un style de vie. Deux espaces d'habitude séparés, comme le salon et le garage, cohabitent naturellement dans une ambiance intermédiaire où, au lieu de réduire les fonctions de chaque zones, des possibilités d'interactions mutuelles sont venues se greffer. En outre, les verrières murales maintiennent la nature comme élément d'ambiance.

Brunete Fraccaroli nahm bei dieser Planung eine extreme Position ein, denn er war der Ansicht, dass man das Haus als Ganzes nutzen sollte. Deshalb entwarf er ein Wohnzimmer, das von einer Garage umgeben ist. An manchen Flächen wurden bunte Schichtplatten angebracht, an anderen Glasscheiben, so dass die Natur zu einem Teil des Wohnraumes wird. Die gesamte Gestaltung ist ein Beispiel dafür, wie man durch die Architektur eine Lebenseinstellung und einen Lebensstil ausdrücken kann. Zwei Räume, die traditionell voneinander getrennt sind, nämlich das Wohnzimmer und die Garage, bestehen auf natürliche Weise nebeneinander und es entstand eine Umgebung, in der die Funktionen der beiden Bereiche nicht eingeschränkt werden, sondern eine Wechselwirkung möglich wurde. Außerdem wurde durch transparente Glaswände die Natur als umgebender Kontext mit einbezogen.

The inner area of the living room, which did not require much natural light, was reserved for impromptu mechanical tasks.

L'intérieur du salon qui n'a pas besoin d'éclairage naturel est réservé pour les travaux de mécanique spontanés.

Im Inneren des Wohnzimmers, wo nicht so viel Tageslicht notwendig ist, befindet sich ein Bereich für spontane, mechanische Arbeiten.

This space, designed in laminated glass, allows its owner to see his sports car at all times.

Le design de cet espace, conçu à base de verre laminé, permet au propriétaire de voir sa voiture de sport à tout moment.

Dieser Raum ist mit beschichtetem Glas so gestaltet, dass der Eigentümer seinen Sportwagen immer sehen kann.

The use of transparent laminated glass integrates nature into the home.

L'emploi de verre laminé transparent permet d'intégrer la nature à l'habitat.

Durch die transparenten, beschichteten Glasflächen wurde auch die Natur in den Wohnraum integriert.

Volumetric Chaos
Chaos de volumes
Chaos der Formen

New York, USA

Though the typical aim of residential architecture is to tame chaos, in the design of this house, Joseph Giovannini let himself be guided by a sort of volumetric chaos that ended up defining the final result of the project. The intention of placing a bedroom in a very small space - which he was averse to compartmentalizing - resulted in a battle for space in which walls bend and flex as if to defend themselves. The materialization of this struggle is a chaotic composition of oblique planes and floating volumes that make up the apartment. The final layout, which conceals the building's thoroughly Cartesian past, refuses to obey any fixed modulation - closets and shelves occupy space in an anarchic fashion. These pieces of furniture are made up of wooden panels and metal sheets, and were designed to force a number of different perspectives and optical illusions that cause the room to expand visually.

A l'ordinaire, l'architecture résidentielle aime à dompter le désordre. Dans ce cas précis, Joseph Giovannini a conçu cette habitation en se laissant guider par l'idée d'un chaos volumétrique pour aboutir au projet final. L'intention d'installer une habitation sur une superficie très réduite, difficile à cloisonner, crée une lutte pour l'espace où les murs se plient et forment des angles comme pour se défendre. Cette bataille se concrétise sous la forme d'une composition désordonnée de plans obliques et de volumes flottants qui finissent par former l'appartement. La distribution finale, qui masque la situation initiale totalement cartésienne, n'obéit à aucune modulation fixe de l'espace, les armoires et les étagères l'occupant de manière anarchique. Ces éléments de mobilier, constitués de panneaux de bois et de lames métalliques, ont été conçus pour créer des perspectives multiples, illusions optiques qui élargissent visuellement l'espace de vie.

Die Wohnhausarchitektur versucht normalerweise, die Unordnung zu bezwingen. Joseph Giovannini hat jedoch ein Wohnhaus entworfen, das von einem Chaos der Formen bestimmt wird, das gleichzeitig zum Endergebnis der Gestaltung wurde. Es sollte Wohnraum auf einer sehr kleinen, kaum zu unterteilenden Fläche geschaffen werden. So kam es zu einem Ringen um Platz, bei dem die Wände sich falten und Winkel bilden. Das Ergebnis dieses Kampfes ist eine ungeordnete Komposition aus schiefen Ebenen und schwebenden Formen, die die Wohnung bilden. Die endgültige Raumaufteilung, die eine völlig kartesianische Vergangenheit verbirgt, unterliegt keiner festen Modulation. Schränke und Regale nehmen den Raum auf anarchische Weise ein. Diese Möbelstücke bestehen aus Holz- und Metallplatten. Sie wurden entworfen, um vielfache Perspektiven und optische Illusionen zu erzeugen, die den Raum visuell vergrößern.

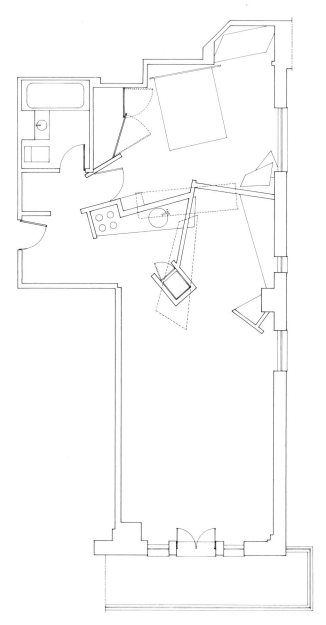

› **Plan** Plan Grundriss

The pristine finish of the chosen materials was brought out using a subtle lighting scheme, which is hidden behind the closets and filters in through cracks and openings.

Les finitions brutes des matériaux sont sublimées par un éclairage subtil caché derrière les armoires et qui s'échappe par des fissures et des renfoncements.

Die makellosen Oberflächen der Materialien wurden durch eine indirekte Beleuchtung unterstrichen, die sich hinter den Schränken versteckt und durch Risse und Vorsprünge entweicht.

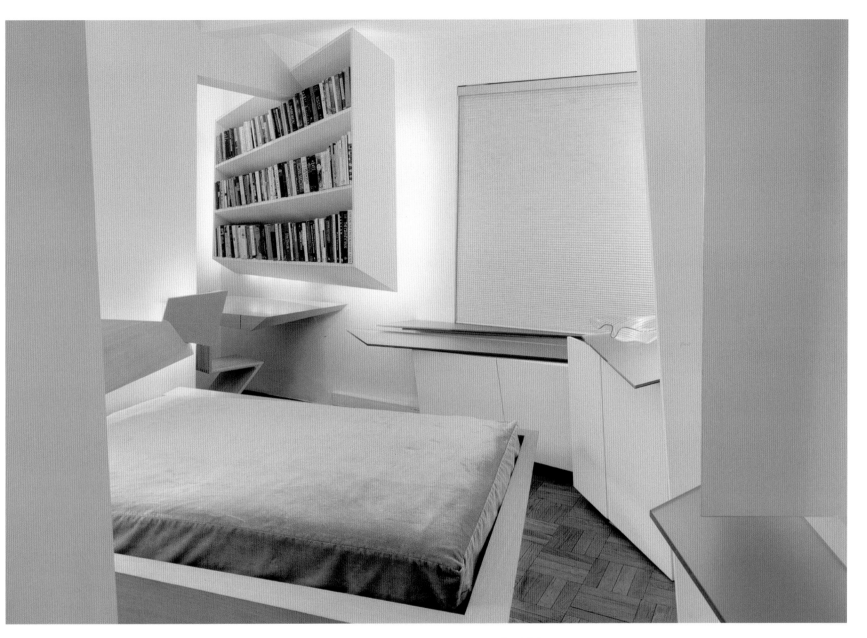

As is the case with most of the furniture, the bookshelf floats on a wall, creating a bewildering sensation of weightlessness.

A l'instar de la grande partie des meubles, la bibliothèque flotte sur un parement provoquant une sensation d'apesanteur troublante.

Wie die meisten anderen Möbel schwebt die Bibliothek über einer Wand, so dass ein verwirrendes Gefühl von Schwerelosigkeit entsteht.

Apartment/Gallery in Berlin
Appartement galerie à Berlin
Appartement-Galerie in Berlin

Berlin, Germany

This project explores multifunctional spaces and boldly suggests that: there can still be a relationship between two spaces given over to entirely opposite functions: living and working. On the one hand, the apartment was required to reserve a specific space for the owner's workshop, and another space - for the gallery - that would be dominated by the aesthetic poetry of the world of art. On the other hand, the floor space given over to domestic use also had to respond to the owner´s inherent needs - hence the multiple references to the art world. This part of the house speaks directly to the senses. The colors, textures, shapes and other elements endow it with a highly personal identity. The mirrors in the living room increase the dimensions of the space, constantly reinterpreting its visual continuity, while, in the gallery, sculptural images seek out a compromise between sensuality and dogmatism.

Ce projet explore la polyvalence spatiale et propose une conception courageuse, la relation entre deux espaces aux fonctions totalement opposées, vivre et travailler. D'un côté, l'appartement devait réserver un espace destiné à la fois à l'activité artistique du propriétaire et à l'installation d'une galerie, une zone envahie de la poésie artistique du monde de l'art. De l'autre, la superficie destinée à l'usage domestique, devait également répondre aux besoins plus intrinsèques du propriétaire, d'où les multiples références au monde artistique. Cette zone parle directement aux sentiments. La couleur, les textures, les formes, tous les éléments dotent l'ensemble d'une identité très personnelle. Les miroirs du salon agrandissent l'espace dans une interprétation de continuité visuelle qui se répète à l'infini. Dans la zone du salon, des représentations sculpturales se scrutent en quête d'un point de rencontre entre sensualité et dogme.

Bei dieser Raumgestaltung wurde mit der Multifunktionalität des Raumes experimentiert und ein gewagter Vorschlag für die Beziehung von zwei Bereichen mit absolut entgegengesetzten Funktionen unterbreitet. In der Wohnung sollte einerseits Raum für die künstlerische Tätigkeit des Eigentümers bleiben, und es sollte eine Galerie entstehen, die von der ästhetischen Poesie der Welt der Kunst erfüllt ist. Andererseits mussten auch die üblichen Wohnfunktionen auf eine Weise vorhanden sein, die dem Charakter des Eigentümers entspricht. Auch die Sinne werden direkt angesprochen. Durch Farben, Texturen, Formen und andere Elemente entstand eine sehr persönliche Umgebung. Die Spiegel im Wohnzimmer vergrößern den Raum und schaffen eine visuelle Kontinuität. Im Ausstellungsbereich erkennt man skulpturelle Bilder, die einen Punkt des Zusammentreffens zwischen dem Sinnlichen und dem Meisterhaften suchen.

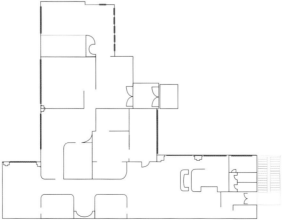

› Plan Plan Grundriss

Candelabras and small complementary lights reinforce the interior lighting scheme and highlight the beauty of the pieces on display.

Chandeliers et sources de lumière complémentaires rehaussent l'éclairage intérieur et subliment la beauté des pièces exposées.

Kandelaber und Lichtquellen ergänzen die Raumbeleuchtung und unterstreichen die Schönheit der ausgestellten Werke.

A bust is the dominant element in the entryway to this gallery area, which focuses on the sensual aspects of individual elements.

La représentation d'un buste préside l'entrée de cette zone d'exposition qui explore la sensualité des éléments.

Eine Büste dominiert den Eingang zum Ausstellungsbereich, und experimentiert gleichzeitig mit der Sinnlichkeit der Elemente.

The vertical walls are white, except for some dashes of color that set off specific pieces of art.

Les parements verticaux sont blancs, sauf à certains endroits où ils changent de couleur pour mettre en valeur une œuvre d'art.

Die vertikalen Wände sind weiß, nur manchmal haben sie eine andere Farbe, um ein Werk des Künstlers zu unterstreichen.

Apartment in South Beach
Appartement à South Beach
Appartement in South Beach

Miami, USA

This 1,600-sq.-ft apartment is located on the second-to-last floor of a futuristic 25-story building. Materials such as marble, steel and glass predominate in this undulating building designed to withstand the hurricanes that periodically besiege Florida's coast. From the entrance, a visitor moves directly to the open living room, and from the living room to the terrace. The curving glass façade offers an impressive panoramic view of the entire city, making it seem like a giant screen. Though lacking a door, the kitchen is still separated from the living room; it is very small and practical, and can also be used as a bar. The interconnection between interior and exterior yields a fluid, contemporary space that takes full advantage of natural light to bring out the massiveness of its structural details. In order to enhance the presence of the exterior inside the apartment, white was chosen as the predominant color for almost the entire house.

Cet appartement de 150 m² se trouve à l'avant dernier étage d'un immeuble futuriste de 25 étages. Les matériaux tels le marbre, l'acier et le verre dominent cet édifice aux lignes incurvées conçu pour résister aux ouragans qui frappent la Floride régulièrement. L'entrée permet d'accéder directement au salon ouvert qui conduit à la terrasse. La façade de verre tout en courbes offre, à l'instar d'un immense écran, une vue panoramique impressionnante sur toute la ville. La cuisine est séparée du salon mais est dépourvue de portes : de petite taille, elle est très pratique et peut également servir de bar. L'interconnexion entre l'intérieur et l'extérieur génère un espace fluide et contemporain qui bénéficie au maximum de la lumière naturelle pour mettre en relief l'ampleur des détails architecturaux. Pour accentuer la présence de l'extérieur à l'intérieur, le choix s'est porté sur le blanc comme couleur présente dans presque tous les décors intérieurs.

Dieses 150 m² große Appartement befindet sich im vorletzten Stockwerk eines futuristischen, 25-stöckigen Gebäudes. Dieses Hochhaus mit seinen gebogenen Linien wird von Materialien wie Marmor, Stahl und Glas dominiert. Die Biegungen dienen dem Schutz vor den Orkanen, die Florida regelmäßig heimsuchen. Vom Eingang aus erreicht man direkt ein offenes Wohnzimmer und dann eine Terrasse. Die gebogene Glasfassade erlaubt einen überwältigenden Blick auf die ganze Stadt, so dass die Wirkung eines enormen Bildschirms entsteht. Die Küche ist vom Wohnzimmer abgetrennt, obwohl es keine Türen gibt. Durch die Verbindung zwischen innen und außen entstand ein fließender Raum, in dem das Tageslicht maximal ausgenutzt wird, um die Größe der konstruktiven Elemente zu unterstreichen. Um die Präsenz der Außenwelt im Inneren noch zu verstärken, wählte man die Farbe Weiß als eine Art Allroundlösung für sämtliche Räume.

The white details defer to the scenery outdoors, which can be seen through an enormous window.

Le blanc des détails constructifs cède son rôle de protagoniste au paysage extérieur qui transparaît au travers des baies vitrées.

Das Weiß der konstruktiven Details überlässt der Außenwelt, die man durch das große Fenster sieht, die Hauptrolle.

Adjacent to the bedroom, a small outdoor terrace ensures that natural light enters the room.

Une petite terrasse extérieure attenante à la chambre à coucher, permet à la lumière naturelle de pénétrer la pièce.

Neben dem Schlafzimmer gibt es eine kleine Terrasse, durch die Licht in den Raum fällt.

Airaghi Residence
Résidence Airaghi
Haus Airaghi

San Francisco, USA

This project responds to the needs of a family who acquired a traditional, two-story Edwardian house and wanted to experiment with a conceptually open dwelling. The new space on the lower floor contains the kitchen, the dining room and a living room replete with tall windows and skylights. A wooden stairway with built-in closets leads to the new, upper floor, which houses the bedrooms and is crowned with a glass skylight. The careful blend of antique and modern elements typifies the design of this house, while the subtlety of some of the decorative details ensures a serene and comfortable interior. A fireplace was installed next to the stairway, which accentuates the verticality of the layout of the interior. The elevated ceiling on the lower floor extends the social spaces outdoors, while the bedroom and bathroom on the upper floor open on to a terrace that offers spectacular views of the city.

Ce projet répond aux besoins d'une famille ayant fait l'acquisition d'une maison traditionnelle de style édouardien à deux étages qu'ils ont transformée en espace ouvert. Le nouveau rez-de-chaussée accueille la cuisine, la salle à manger et un salon doté de fenêtres tout en hauteur et de velux pour laisser entrer la lumière. Un escalier de bois agrémenté d'armoires intégrées dessert le nouvel étage hébergeant les chambres, couronné par une verrière. L'association bien étudiée d'éléments anciens et modernes définit le design de cette habitation. La subtilité de certains détails décoratifs permet d'obtenir un intérieur où règnent sérénité et confort. Une cheminée s'élève à côté de l'escalier, soulignant ainsi la verticalité de la distribution intérieure. La toiture élevée du rez-de-chaussée prolonge les espaces de réception vers l'extérieur, tandis que la chambre à coucher et la salle de bains de l'étage supérieur s'ouvrent sur une terrasse avec des vues spectaculaires sur la ville.

Die Kunden erwarben ein traditionelles, zweistöckiges Haus im Edward-Stil und wünschten, mit dem Konzept eines offenen Wohnraums zu experimentieren. In dem neu gestalteten Raum im Erdgeschoss befinden sich die Küche, das Esszimmer und das Wohnzimmer mit seinen hohen Fenstern und Dachfenstern, durch die viel Licht fällt. Eine Holztreppe mit eingebauten Schränken führt in das neue Stockwerk mit den Schlafzimmern, das von einem Dachfenster aus Glas gekrönt wird. Die gelungene Mischung alter und moderner Elemente definiert die Gestaltung dieses Wohnhauses. An der Treppe befindet sich ein Kamin, der die Vertikalität der Raumaufteilung unterstreicht. Das erhöhte Dach des Erdgeschosses verlängert die Wohnräume nach außen, während das Schlafzimmer und das Bad im ersten Stock sich zu einer Terrasse mit einem wundervollen Blick über die Stadt öffnen.

The stairway, which includes built-in storage space at its lower end, dominates the main space in the house; adjacent to it, a fireplace and chimney accentuate the height of the ceilings.

L'escalier, doté d'armoires dans sa partie inférieure, domine l'espace principal. Une cheminée attenante s'élève, accentuant la hauteur du toit.

Die Treppe, in die unten Schränke eingebaut sind, beherrscht das Bild. Daneben erhebt sich ein Kamin, der die Höhe der Decke unterstreicht.

The versatility offered by an open plan was maximized throughout. The kitchen, dining room and living room share a single space on the lower floor.

La polyvalence de l'intérieur ouvert a été optimisée. La cuisine, la salle à manger et le salon partagent le même espace au rez-de-chaussée.

Die Vielseitigkeit der offenen Räume wurde so weit wie möglich optimiert. Die Küche, das Speisezimmer und das Wohnzimmer befinden sich im gleichen Raum im Erdgeschoss.

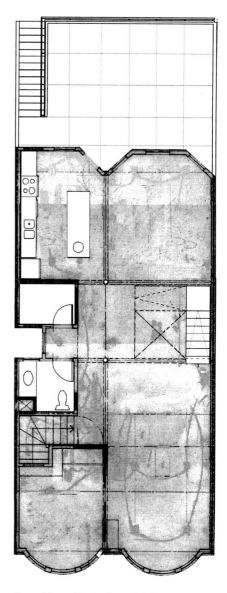

› Ground floor Rez-de-chaussée Erdgeschoss

Some of the original details - such as the wrought iron columns - were preserved.

Certains détails originaux, à l'instar des colonnes de fer forgé, ont été conservés.

Einige der Originalelemente wie die Säulen aus Schmiedeeisen blieben erhalten.

The skylights and windows on the new floor - which houses the kitchen and the bedrooms - allow for a bright, transparent interior.

Les velux et fenêtres du nouvel étage, où se trouvent la cuisine et les chambres, permettent de créer un intérieur lumineux et transparent.

Die Dachfenster und Fenster des neuen Stockwerks, in dem sich die Küche und Schlafzimmer befinden, lassen viel Licht in die Räume.

Eric' Apartment
Appartement Eric
Appartement Eric

Miami, USA

This 3,750-sq.-ft apartment is located on the 23rd floor of a skyscraper in South Beach, overlooking the Atlantic Ocean. Its spacious terrace is covered by a roof and opens directly on to the living room, thanks to two large sliding doors. The owners of the apartment use it for open-air dining. The enormous mirror hung on the corner of the wall delimiting the dining room reflects the city as if it were a painting or large window. The decor emulates the nostalgic style typical of 1960s Miami - white, white and white - throughout. Inside, both the versatility of this open space and the entrance of natural light were optimized. The living room and bedroom both open on to the terrace. Thanks to the continuity of the flooring materials used throughout, the various areas of the house seem to be unconstrained; different functional uses are confused and the dimensions of the apartment seem to increase.

Cet appartement de 350 m² est situé au 23e étage d'un gratte-ciel de South Beach avec vues sur la mer. La vaste terrasse est en partie couverte et communique directement avec le salon grâce à deux grandes portes coulissantes. Les propriétaires l'utilisent pour déjeuner en plein air. L'immense miroir installé dans un coin de la salle à manger, reflète la ville, à l'instar d'un grand tableau ou d'une grande fenêtre. Toute la décoration intérieure conserve le style nostalgique en blanc typique du Miami des années soixante. A l'intérieur, la polyvalence d'un espace ouvert et l'entrée de la lumière naturelle ont été optimisés. La sérénité du blanc et l'uniformité des finitions accroissent la sensation d'ampleur et dynamise l'espace intérieur. Le salon et la chambre à coucher s'ouvrent sur la terrasse. Grâce à la continuité du carrelage, l'espace semble illimité, les fonctions fusionnent et accroissent la dimension réelle de l'appartement.

Dieses 350 m² große Appartement befindet sich im 23. Stock eines Wolkenkratzers in South Beach mit Blick aufs Meer. Die große Terrasse ist teilweise überdacht und direkt durch zwei große Schiebetüren mit dem Wohnzimmer verbunden. Die Eigentümer pflegen dort im Freien zu speisen. Ein riesiger Spiegel an der Ecke, die als Essecke dient, reflektiert die Stadt und wirkt wie ein Gemälde oder ein großes Fenster. Die gesamte Innendekoration hat den nostalgischen, weißen Stil bewahrt, der typisch für das Miami der Siebzigerjahre war. Im Inneren wurde die Vielseitigkeit des offenen Raumes optimiert und es fällt viel Tageslicht herein. Durch die Gelassenheit der Farbe Weiß und die Einheitlichkeit der Oberflächen wird Eindruck von Weite verstärkt und der Raum wirkt dynamisch. Das Wohn- und das Schlafzimmer öffnen sich zur Terrasse. Durch den einheitlichen Bodenbelag scheinen die Bereiche unbegrenzt zu sein. Die Nutzungsarten vermischen sich und die Wohnung wirkt noch größer.

The furniture and finishing respect the idea of uniformity throughout the house.

Le choix du mobilier et des finitions respecte le concept d'uniformité de l'ensemble de l'habitation.

Die Auswahl der Möbel und Oberflächen entspricht dem Konzept der Einheitlichkeit in der ganzen Wohnung.

All the walls, furniture, and floors were finished in white to achieve a serene and light-filled interior.

Le blanc couvre tous les parements, le mobilier et le sol pour obtenir un intérieur serein et lumineux.

Alle Wände, Möbel und Böden sind in weiß gehalten, so dass eine gelassene und helle Umgebung entstand.

The living room is open to the outside thanks to sliding doors, which allow natural light to invade the rest of the rooms.

Le salon s'ouvre sur l'extérieur grâce à des portes coulissantes permettant à la lumière naturelle d'inonder le reste de l'espace de vie.

Die großen Schiebetüren des Wohnzimmers, durch die Licht in alle Räume fällt, können geöffnet werden.

The bedroom also opens on to the outdoor terrace, which is used for eating in the open air.

La chambre est dotée d'un accès à la terrasse extérieure, utilisée pour prendre les repas en plein air.

Vom Schlafzimmer aus gelangt man ebenfalls auf die Außenterrasse, die als Speisezimmer im Freien dient.

Penthouse in New York
Attique à New-York
Penthouse in New York

New York, USA

This apartment with a terrace is located on the 22nd floor of a residential tower. The clients, a young couple, wanted an open, serene space that would also meet all their needs. The firm that carried out the design decided to lay out the main spaces - living room, kitchen, dining room, office, and bedroom - in linear fashion along the side of the building opening on to the terrace, so that all these rooms would receive plenty of natural light. The other service areas, such as the bathroom, toilet, and storage room, were relegated to the opposite side of the apartment, making the rational organization of the interior apparent. Light, materials, colors, and textures are mixed in order to accentuate the visual and tactile perception of this space as a loft. Outside, the small stone fountain and the use of materials such as ebony, create a relaxed atmosphere that exudes calm and well-being.

Cette habitation avec terrasse est située au 22e étage d'un immeuble résidentiel. Les clients, un jeune couple, désiraient un espace ouvert et serein répondant à tous leurs besoins. L'entreprise chargée de la conception a opté pour la disposition en enfilade des espaces principaux- salon, cuisine, salle à manger, bureau et chambre à coucher- adossés à la façade ouverte sur la terrasse, de sorte que l'ensemble des espaces bénéficie de la lumière naturelle. Par contre, d'autres aires de service à l'instar de la salle de bains, des toilettes et d'une pièce arrière sont reléguées sur le côté opposé de l'appartement. On obtient ainsi un intérieur organisé de manière rationnelle. La lumière, les matériaux, les couleurs et les textures se mêlent pour accentuer la perception visuelle et tactile du loft. A l'extérieur, l'emploi de matériaux comme le bois d'ébène ou la pierre du petit jet d'eau, contribue à créer une ambiance détendue empreinte de calme et de bien-être.

Diese Dachwohnung mit Terrasse befindet sich im 22. Stockwerk eines Wohngebäudes. Die Kunden, ein junges Paar, wünschten sich einen offenen und ruhig wirkenden Raum, der all ihre Bedürfnisse erfüllt. Das Unternehmen, das die Gestaltung übernahm, ordnete die wichtigsten Räume, also Wohnzimmer, Küche, Speisezimmer, Büro und Schlafzimmer linear entlang der Fassade an. Daran schließt sich eine Terrasse an, so dass in alle Räume Tageslicht fällt. Andere Räume wie das Bad, die Toilette und eine Abstellkammer liegen auf der anderen Seite der Wohnung. So wurden die Räume rationell geordnet. Das Licht, die Materialien, die Farben und die Texturen vermischen sich, um die visuelle und haptische Wahrnehmung des Lofts unterstreichen. Außen tragen Materialien wie Ebenholz und der Stein der kleinen Wasserfontaine zu einer entspannten Atmosphäre von Ruhe und Wohlbefinden bei.

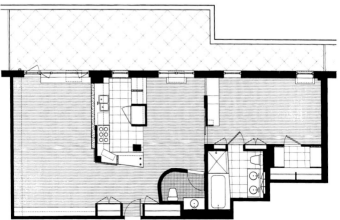

› Plan Plan Grundriss

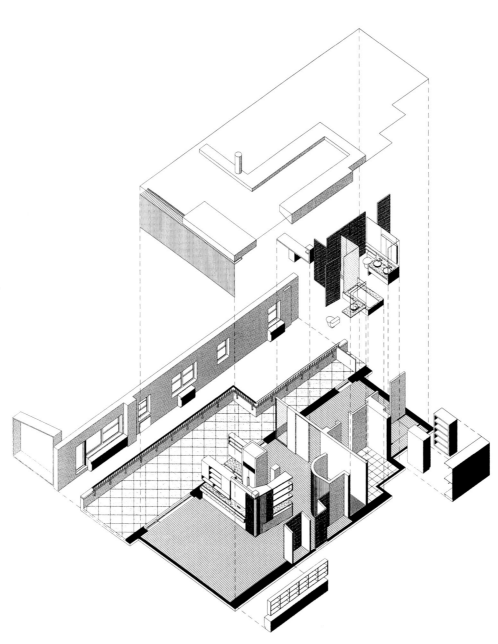

› Axonometric view   Axonométrie   Axonometrische Ansicht

Apartment in Sydney
Appartement à Sydney
Appartement in Sydney

Sydney, Australia

The organization of this apartment revolves around a pivoting dining room table that can spin 180 degrees - it can thus be swung into the kitchen, the studio, or around to the living room. This table pivots on a column that replaced an original load-bearing wall; its steel structure holds up a nine-foot-long glass plate that weighs 220 pounds. In the bedroom, a set of sliding doors made of a bluish translucent resin provides views of the sea from the bed. An electronically-activated video projection system guarantees darkness at night by blocking the light that filters in through the windows. To emphasize the spectacular views, the materials used in the apartment differ in brightness and transparency. The bright finishes, such as the floor or the table, introduce sea and sky tones into the interior of the dwelling, which incidentally has over 60 individual light fixtures.

L'organisation de cet appartement s'articule autour d'une table de salle à manger pivotante à 180 degrés. Elle peut être située tant dans la cuisine que dans le bureau ou le salon. La table pivote sur une colonne qui remplace le mur portant d'origine et dispose d'une structure d'acier inoxydable qui soutient une plaque de verre de 3 m de long, pesant 100 kilos. Dans la chambre à coucher, des portes coulissantes en résine translucide bleue permettent de profiter des vues sur la mer depuis le lit. Une projection vidéo à commande électrique maintient l'obscurité pendant la nuit en bloquant la lumière qui filtre par les baies vitrées. Pour rehausser l'impact des vues, les matériaux utilisés dans l'appartement diffèrent en luminosité et transparence. Les finitions lumineuses, à l'instar du carrelage ou de la table, introduisent les couleurs du ciel et de la mer à l'intérieur de cette habitation, qui compte plus de 60 points d'éclairage.

Bei der Raumaufteilung dieses Appartements wurde ein Esstisch, der um 180 Grad gedreht werden und sich so entweder in der Küche, im Büro oder im Wohnzimmer befinden kann, als Ausgangspunkt genommen. Er dreht sich auf einer Säule, die die ursprüngliche tragende Wand ersetzt und die ein Struktursystem aus Edelstahl besitzt, das eine 3 m lange und 100 kg schwere Glasplatte trägt. Im Schlafzimmer ermöglichen es Schiebetüren aus durchscheinendem, bläulichen Kunstharz, dass man vom Bett aus aufs Meer schauen kann. Eine elektrische Steuerung sorgt nachts für Dunkelheit, indem das Licht, abgeschirmt wird. Um den beeindruckenden Ausblick zu unterstreichen, wurden Materialien verwendet, die sich in ihrer Helligkeit und Transparenz unterscheiden. Glänzende Flächen wie der Bodenbelag und der Tisch bringen die Farben des Himmels und des Meeres in die Wohnung, in der es über 60 Lichtquellen gibt.

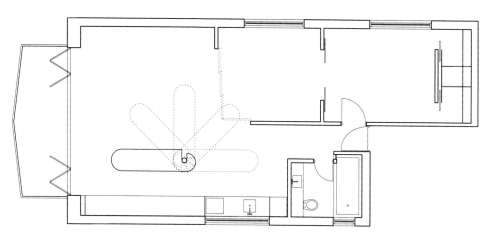

› Plan Plan Grundriss

As enclosing the work area would have kept the table from spinning all the way around, a system of sliding panels was designed to make it easier to open.

Vu que la délimitation de la zone de travail aurait pu empêcher d'installer la table, la conception d'un système de panneaux coulissants en facilite l'ouverture.

Um zu vermeiden, dass die Bewegung des Tisches behindert wird, wurde ein System aus gleitenden Paneelen entwickelt, mit dem man den Arbeitsbereich öffnen kann.

Franc Fernández

Barcelona, Spain

Home in Barcelona
Habitation à Barcelone
Wohnung Barcelona

The renovation of this building - originally a factory - led to its being put to residential use. Leaving the 18-foot ceilings intact preserved the industrial feel and also served to bestow a unique personality on the new residences. This apartment has the advantage of occupying a corner of the building, and so enjoys abundant natural light. The existing structure was maintained to some extent: the metal beams and columns, the tiled vaulting, and even the large original windows were all preserved. The floor space was divided into two areas: the first groups the kitchen, dining room, and living room into one large space, and the second contains the bedroom, bathroom, toilet, and studio. The first area, which is more public, maintains the original high ceilings and enjoys a substantial amount of natural light. The second, however, was supplemented with an intermediate structure that divides it into spaces of differing heights.

La réhabilitation de cet édifice a restructuré l'usine qu'il abritait au départ en une résidence. Les 4,50 m de hauteur du projet initial, laissés intacts, perpétuent le caractère des lieux, conférant aux nouvelles habitations une personnalité très marquée. Cet appartement a l'avantage d'occuper un angle de l'édifice, profitant ainsi de toute la lumière naturelle nécessaire. La structure préexistante conserve certains des détails constructifs antérieurs : les poutres maîtresses et piliers métalliques, le forgeage d'entrevous en céramiques et même les grandes verrières d'origine. L'étage est divisé en deux zones : d'un côté, la cuisine, la salle à manger et le salon réunis en un seul espace, et de l'autre la chambre à coucher, la salle de bains, les toilettes et le bureau. La première partie, la moins privée, conserve la hauteur des toits et bénéficie en grande partie de la lumière naturelle. La deuxième, en revanche, a été complétée par un lattis intermédiaire, qui partage l'espace dans sa hauteur.

In einem ehemaligen Fabrikgebäude wurden Wohnungen geschaffen, in denen man die Originalhöhe von 4,50 m beibehielt und so den industriellen Charakter des Gebäudes unterstrich. Diese Wohnung befindet sich an einer Ecke des Gebäudes, so dass besonders viel Tageslicht in die Räume fällt. Man behielt einige der Baumerkmale der Originalstruktur wie die Tragbalken und die Säulen aus Metall, die Keramikstruktur der Gewölbe und die riesigen Fenster bei. Die Räume wurden in zwei Bereiche unterteilt. In einem der beiden Bereiche befinden sich in einem einzigen Raum die Küche, das Speisezimmer und das Esszimmer, in dem anderen das Schlafzimmer, das Bad, die Toilette und das Atelier. Im ersten Raum, der weniger privat ist, wurden die hohen Decken erhalten und es fällt viel Licht ein. Im zweiten Bereich wurde jedoch ein Mauerwerk eingezogen, das die Höhe des Raumes unterteilt.

Spaciousness, light, and versatility were the goals in designing this industrial space.

Amplitude, luminosité et polyvalence sont les objectifs de cet espace industriel.

Weite, Helligkeit und Vielseitigkeit wurden zu den Ausgangspunkten der Planung in diesem Fabrikgebäude.

Apartment in Manhattan
Appartement à Manhattan
Appartement in Manhattan

New York, USA

The main goal in designing this 2,000-sq.-ft apartment was to detect in advance whichever issues would require specific solutions. Thus, the main objectives were to integrate the overall design into the city, to take full advantage of the four sides of the building and the roof, and to provide space for a collection of furniture and decorative art by 20th-century artists and architects. On the lower level of the apartment, the public and private spheres are clearly differentiated. The area designed for social gatherings occupies the south façade and is organized around an element shaped like a water tank. A large living room - with a fireplace - and a dining room - with an adjacent sitting room - are located on opposite sides of the central artifact, a space that resembles a glass box containing a stainless-steel staircase shaped like a double helix. The sequence of slide windows creates a setting flooded with light.

Cet appartement de 200 m² ou presque suit un processus dont l'objectif est de trouver une solution concrète aux problèmes qui pourraient surgir. Les priorités suivantes ont été fixées : intégrer le projet à la ville, optimiser au maximum les quatre façades et la couverture et abriter la collection de meubles et d'œuvres d'art décoratif d'artistes et d'architectes du XXe siècle. Au niveau inférieur de l'appartement, les sphères publiques et privées sont clairement définies. La zone destinée aux réunions sociales occupe la façade sud et s'articule autour d'un élément intérieur en forme de récipient d'eau. Un grand salon doté d'une cheminée et salle à manger avec une zone attenante pour s'asseoir se trouvent de chaque côté de l'artefact central -un espace qui ressemble à un cube de verre doté d'un double escalier hélicoïdal d'acier inoxydable. L'enfilade de fenêtres latérales crée un espace intérieur lumineux et fluide.

Als man diese fast 200 m² große Wohnung plante, wurden zuerst die Punkte analysiert, für die eine konkrete Lösung notwendig war. So legte man als Prioritäten fest, die Wohnung in die Stadt zu integrieren, die vier Fassaden und die Decke so gut wie möglich auszunutzen und einen Platz für die dekorativen Möbel und Kunstwerke von Künstlern und Architekten des 20. Jh. zu schaffen. In der unteren Etage der Wohnung sind die privaten und gemeinschaftlichen Bereiche klar voneinander getrennt. Der Bereich für Zusammenkünfte liegt an der Südfassade und im Zentrum dieser Zone ein Element, das die Form eines Wassertanks hat. Ein großes Wohnzimmer mit Kamin und ein Esszimmer mit anliegender Sitzecke befinden sich auf beiden Seiten des zentralen Körpers, ein Raum, der wie ein Glaskasten aussieht und in dem sich eine Edelstahltreppe mit doppelter Spirale befindet. Durch die nebeneinander liegenden Fenstern an den Seiten fällt viel Licht ein.

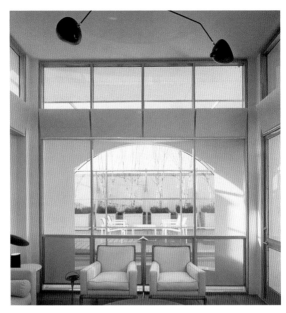

The idea of conceiving a space emanating calm was achieved by using contemporary, functional furniture.

La conception d'un espace imprégné de tranquillité a pu être réalisée en employant un mobilier contemporain et fonctionnel.

Es sollte ein Raum entstehen, der Ruhe ausstrahlt. Erreicht wurde dies durch moderne und funktionelle Möbel.

An arching steel beam holds up the steps of the staircase, which leads to the upper part of the residence.

Une voûte d'acier soutient les marches de l'escalier qui conduisent à la partie supérieure.

Eine Arkade aus Stahl hält die Stufen der Treppe, die nach oben führt.

T House
Maison T
Haus T

Kloten, Switzerland

The architects of this house describe it as two independent pieces that were joined to form a single living space that is both spacious and filled with light. To achieve this, the building was gutted to its foundations, and a longitudinal axis was introduced in the upper part of the house; this serves to articulate the various spaces making up the house. A double-height gallery links the two floors, as wella as displaying a delicate metal staircase that appears almost to be a sculpture. This stair doubles as a divider between the living room and the library. A limited range of materials and colors - used in strict separation - enhance this notion of space. The floor on the lower level, which is open to the public, is tiled in sandstone, while the private upstairs section is floored in parquet. The beige walls, whose colos falls halfway between that of the stone and the wooden floors upstairs, create an overall feeling of peace.

Les architectes ont conçu le projet en deux parties dotées de fonctions indépendantes, réunies en une seule habitation, ample et lumineuse. Cela étant, la construction a été vidée jusqu'aux fondations pour introduire un axe longitudinal dans la partie supérieure distribuant les différents espaces de l'habitation. Une galerie à double hauteur réunit les deux étages de la maison. Elle héberge un escalier métallique tout en finesse, perçu à la fois comme une sculpture et un élément séparateur entre le salon et la bibliothèque. Une parcimonie de matériaux et de couleurs, séparés les uns des autres, définit cette idée de l'espace. Le carrelage du rez-de-chaussée, à usage public, est en grés, tandis qu'à l'étage supérieur, réservé aux zones privées, le sol est recouvert de parquet. Le beige des murs, à mi-chemin entre la couleur de la pierre et du bois, crée un effet monolithique empreint d'une grande sérénité.

Die Architekten beschreiben dieses Gebäude als zwei Hälften, die unabhängig voneinander funktionieren, und aus denen man eine einzige, weite und helle Wohnung gemacht hat. Dazu wurde das Gebäude bis auf die Grundmauern geleert und eine Längsachse im oberen Teil eingeführt. Eine Galerie in doppelter Höhe verbindet die beiden Etagen des Hauses. Auf dieser Galerie befindet sich eine feine Metalltreppe, die wie eine Skulptur wahrgenommen wird und gleichzeitig das Wohnzimmer von der Bibliothek trennt. Diese Raumidee wird von wenig Farben, die voneinander getrennt sind, begleitet. Der Boden des Erdgeschosses ist aus Sandstein, während der Boden des Obergeschosses, in dem sich die Privaträume befinden, mit Holzparkett belegt ist. Die Wände sind beige, die Farbe vermittelt zwischen der des Steines und der des Holzes. So entsteht eine sehr einheitlich wirkende und somit beruhigende Atmosphäre.

The upper floor, which contains the private areas of the home, is floored in parquet.

Le sol de l'étage supérieur, où se trouvent les sphères privées, est revêtu de parquet.

Der Boden im Obergeschoss, in dem die privaten Räume liegen, ist mit Parkett belegt.

A one-piece module in the middle of the kitchen adds a professional touch to the ensemble.

Un module d'une seule pièce, mis en exergue au cœur de la cuisine, confère à l'ensemble un aspect professionnel.

Mitten in der Küche fällt ein Modul aus einem einzigen Teil auf, das der Küche einen professionellen Touch gibt.

Studio in Turin
Studio à Turin
Kleine Wohnung in Turin

Turin, Italy

As the clients wanted to get the most out of this small studio, they inserted a second level so that the total floor area was increased to 960 square ft. The aim was to create a highly organized house that would exhibit a hierarchy of spaces and domestic functions. Two bedrooms were placed on the lower level, along with their respective bathrooms and a service room. The upper level was given over to daytime activities: the kitchen, pantry, living room and dining room were set here. All the spaces in the house, except for those used for storage, combined to form a larger, single space, enhancing the overall sensation of spaciousness. This multifunctional space is illuminated by a large window that opens automatically and floods the lower level with light. The stairway that connects the two levels is the central focus of the composition, as it ties together the two levels of the house and opens the lower one to natural light.

Les clients ont voulu optimiser au maximum la surface réduite de ce studio, en concevant deux niveaux dont la superficie est de 90 m². L'organisation de l'habitation est très précise suivant un schéma spatial et fonctionnel parfaitement hiérarchisé. Le premier niveau accueille les chambres à coucher et les salles de bains attenantes ainsi qu'une pièce de service. Le niveau supérieur est réservé aux activités de jour : la cuisine, une réserve, le salon et la salle à manger. Tous les espaces, à l'exception de la pièce de rangement, forment un espace unique, ce qui confère à l'habitat une sensation d'ampleur. En outre, cet étage polyvalent est illuminé par une grande verrière qui s'ouvre grâce à une commande, baignant ainsi l'étage inférieur de lumière naturelle. L'escalier, qui relie les deux niveaux, est l'axe névralgique du projet : il est le trait d'union entre les deux espaces et permet à la lumière naturelle d'inonder l'espace.

Die Kunden wünschten sich, den wenigen vorhandenen Platz so gut wie möglich auszunutzen. Deshalb wurden zwei Ebenen geschaffen, deren Fläche zusammen 90 m² ergeben. Auf der unteren Ebene liegen zwei Schlafzimmer mit ihren Bädern und der Waschküche. Auf der oberen Ebene finden die Aktivitäten des Tages statt. Hier liegen die Küche, die Speisekammer, das Wohnzimmer und das Esszimmer. Alle Räume bis auf den Lagerraum sind in einen einzigen Raum integriert, so dass die Wohnung viel größer wirkt als sie ist. Diese multifunktionelle Ebene erhält durch ein großes Fenster, das man mit einem elektrischen Mechanismus öffnen kann, sehr viel Tageslicht, das auch in die untere Ebene fällt. Die Treppe zwischen den beiden Ebenen ist ein sehr wichtiges Element, das die beiden Etagen miteinander verbindet und das Tageslicht durchlässt.

On its lower stretches, the stairway 's metal structure incorporates beechwood risers; higher up, these give way to sandblasted glass steps.

La structure métallique de l'escalier soutient, au départ, un tronçon de marches en bois de bouleau, et un deuxième tronçon de marches en verre traité au jet de sable.

Die Metallstruktur der Treppe hält im ersten Abschnitt zwei Stufen aus Birkenholz, und im zweiten Abschnitt Stufen aus sandgestrahltem Glas.

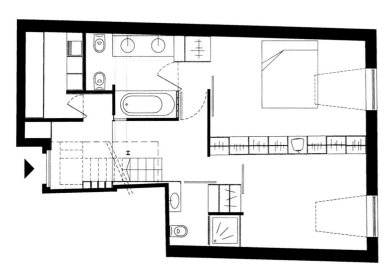

› Lower floor   Etage inférieur   Untergeschoss

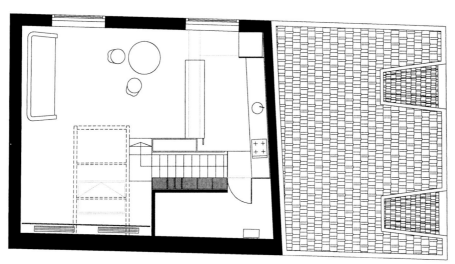

› Upper floor   Etage supérieur   Obergeschoss

Loft in New York
Loft à New York
Loft in New York

New York, USA

This design entailed converting an industrial space into a loft-style home. The primary objective was to maintain the magnificent panoramic views enjoyed, as well as the existing sources of natural light. A layer of concrete was poured over the floor to achieve acoustical insulation for the lower level. The designers strived to use as few partitions as possible, and a false ceiling was installed; this proved to be highly useful for installing part of the lighting system. The layout focuses on two central volumes containing two bathrooms and a studio, and are additionally enveloped by a light skin of wood and glass that allows natural light to filter through. The positioning of these two volumes reveals the space in its entirety, though they also serve to outline and grant additional privacy to certain areas and to make the interior layout more interesting.

Le projet consiste à réhabiliter un espace industriel en une habitation. Le premier objectif est de conserver les superbes vues panoramiques et les sources de lumière naturelle préexistantes au départ. En outre, le sol est revêtu d'une couche de béton uniforme pour égaliser les niveaux et créer une isolation phonique avec l'étage supérieur. Les cloisonnements ont été éliminés au maximum, un faux plafond a été installé pour résoudre certains détails d'éclairage. L'organisation spatiale s'articule autour de deux corps centraux, contenant deux salles de bains et un bureau. Ils sont enveloppés d'une fine membrane de bois et verre permettant à la lumière naturelle d'inonder le loft. La position de ces deux volumes permet de percevoir l'ensemble de l'espace tout en préservant l'intimité nécessaire à certaines sphères et générant un parcours intérieur intéressant.

Ein industrieller Raum sollte zu einer Wohnung umgestaltet werden. Dabei sollten der wundervolle Panoramablick und die Tatsache, dass reichlich Tageslicht in den leeren Raum strömte, nicht beeinträchtigt werden. Der Boden wurde mit einer einheitlichen Betonschicht überzogen, um ihn zu begradigen. Man versuchte, den Raum so wenig wie möglich zu unterteilen und zog eine praktische Zwischendecke ein, die als Träger für einige Beleuchtungselemente dient. Der Raum wurde um zwei zentrale Körper herum aufgeteilt, in denen zwei Bäder und ein Atelier liegen. Sie sind von einer leichten Haut aus Holz und Glas umgeben, durch die Licht einfällt. Die Anordnung dieser beiden Körper ermöglicht eine Gesamtwahrnehmung des Raumes, aber gleichzeitig werden die Räumlichkeiten begrenzt und in bestimmten Zonen die Privatsphäre geschützt. Es entstand eine interessante innere Struktur.

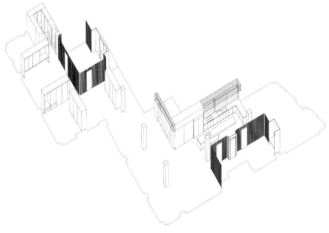

› Axonometric view   Axonométrie   Axonometrische Ansicht

The space is structured around two volumes that contain the bathrooms and are enveloped by a thin wooden membrane.

Deux corps, enveloppés d'une fine membrane de bois, contenant les salles de bain structurent l'espace.

Der Raum wird von zwei Körpern strukturiert, die von einer leichten Haut aus Holz umhüllt sind und in denen sich die Bäder befinden.

The use of closely-spaced, thin slats of wood alongside glass allows natural light to enter the more private spaces in the house.

L'emploi de fines lamelles boisées entrecoupées de verre permet de faire entrer la lumière naturelle dans les zones à l'abri des regards indiscrets.

Die Verwendung von schmalen, mit Abstand verlegten Holzplatten und von Glas machte es möglich, dass Tageslicht auch in die von Blicken abgeschirmten Bereiche fällt.

Steel Loft
Loft Steel
Steel Loft

New York, USA

For this loft, the architects came up with a spatial concept that could be modulated and articulated hierarchically by means of vertical and horizontal panels and layers. Conceptually, the design was based on a three-dimensional reinterpretation of a painting by Mondrian, in which a system of lines gives rise to different spaces; while still being seen as a whole. Two circulation areas determine the way in which the inhabitants of the loft move through it: the first, defined by the space created between a row of columns, links the kitchen, dining room, living room and television room. The second runs along the edge parallel to the façade and connects the studio with the main bedroom. This circulation system, along with the ensemble of panels and partitions, separates domestic functions without compartmentalizing the house. The only doors in the house belong to the bedrooms and bathrooms.

L'objectif des architectes était de parvenir à une vision spatiale modulable qui puisse s'articuler selon une hiérarchie grâce à des panneaux et couches verticaux et horizontaux. La conception des architectes repose sur la ré-interprétation en trois dimensions d'un tableau de Mondrian, dans lequel un système linéaire crée des espaces différents tout en faisant partie d'un ensemble. Deux zones de circulation organisent le déplacement des habitants du loft. La première, définie par la superficie créée entre une enfilade de colonnes, connecte la cuisine, la salle à manger, le salon et la salle de télévision. La seconde parcourt la frange parallèle à la façade et permet d'aller du bureau à la chambre à coucher principale. Ce système de circulation permet de séparer les diverses fonctions domestiques sans compartimenter l'habitation. Seules les chambres et les salles de bains disposent de portes coulissantes pour les premières et fixes pour les secondes.

Ziel der Architekten war es, eine räumliche Vision zu schaffen, die hierarchisch durch vertikale und horizontale Platten und Schichten moduliert und gegliedert wird. Grundlage des Konzeptes der Architekten war die dreidimensionale Neuinterpretation eines Werkes von Mondrian, in dem ein System aus Linien unterschiedliche Räume formt, die jedoch ein Ganzes bilden. Die Bewohner des Lofts bewegen sich über zwei dafür geschaffene Zonen. Die erste ist die Fläche, die zwischen einer Reihe von Säulen entstanden ist und die die Küche, das Speisezimmer, das Wohnzimmer und den Fernsehraum miteinander verbindet. Die zweite Zone verläuft parallel zur Fassade und man gelangt zum Atelier oder zum Schlafzimmer. Durch dieses System der Verbindung und die Paneele und Raumteiler wurden die verschiedenen Wohnfunktionen voneinander abgetrennt, ohne dass die Wohnung unterteilt wirkt. Nur an den Schlafzimmern und Bädern gibt es Türen.

A row of columns fifteen feet away from the façade serves to link the living room, dining room, and kitchen.

Une enfilade de colonnes à cinq mètres de la façade, forme le trait d'union entre le salon, la salle à manger et la cuisine.

Eine Säulenreihe, die sich 5 Meter von der Fassade entfernt befindet, wird zum Verbindungselement zwischen dem Wohnzimmer, dem Esszimmer und der Küche.

Large spaces allow natural light to flood every room, further enhancing the overall visual continuity.

Les vastes espaces permettent à la lumière de parcourir tous les espaces de vie de l'habitation, favorisant la continuité visuelle de l'ensemble.

Durch die weiten Räume fällt das Tageslicht überall hin und die visuelle Kontinuität wird verstärkt.

The central space is bright and free of obstacles; it is separated from the rest of the home by partitions that do not reach the ceiling.

L'espace central, libre et diaphane, est séparé du reste par des cloisons qui ne vont pas jusqu'au plafond.

Der zentrale Raum wirkt frei und transparent und wird von den übrigen Räumen mit Raumteilern abgetrennt, die nicht bis zur Decke reichen.

Apartment in London
Appartement à Londres
Appartement in London

London, UK

This apartment, which was originally built without a roof, was transformed into a cozy home in which its owners could take refuge from the stresses of city life. Its main assets, which were highlighted by the renovation, were abundant natural light and stunning views. One of the main challenges was to facilitate mobility through the apartment, in such a way that the lighting or structure of the homes various areas could be altered without any significant effort. To this end, the architect used individual light fixtures that permitted an easy interplay of lights, as well as decorative elements such as curtains, which soften the natural light filtering through them. The stairway and living room are joined by a wooden door that spins 360 degrees on a central axis. The stainless-steel kitchen gives the house an industrial look, while the variety of materials adapted to suit each space enriches the overall atmosphere of the apartment.

Cet appartement, constitué à l'origine d'une ancienne structure dépourvue de toit, a été réhabilité en habitation accueillante pour échapper à l'agitation urbaine. Lors de la restauration, les points forts, à l'instar de la lumière naturelle et des vues magnifiques, ont été particulièrement mis en valeur. Rendre à cet appartement une impression de mobilité a été l'un des défis principaux à relever, en modifiant facilement l'éclairage ou la structure des ambiances. A cette fin, l'architecte a opté pour l'emploi de points d'éclairage, créant facilement des jeux de lumière ou pour des éléments décoratifs, à l'instar de rideaux, pour diminuer l'incidence de la lumière naturelle sur l'intérieur. L'escalier et le salon sont reliés par une porte giratoire en bois sur un axe central qui pivote de 360 degrés. La cuisine en acier inoxydable accentue l'aspect industriel. Le mélange de matériaux qui s'adaptent aux caractéristiques de chaque espace, sublime l'atmosphère générale.

Diese Wohnung, die ehemals als eine Struktur ohne Decke konstruiert war, wurde in eine einladende Wohnung umgebaut, in der man sich von der Hektik der Stadt erholen kann. Beim Umbau wurde besonders darauf geachtet, dass weiterhin viel Tageslicht einfallen konnte und der wundervolle Blick nicht versperrt wurde. Eines der Hauptziele war es, die Wohnung flexibel zu machen, so dass die Beleuchtung und die Raumaufteilung ohne großen Aufwand verändert werden können. Dazu wählte der Architekt einfache Lichtquellen und Dekorationselemente wie Gardinen, durch die gedämpftes Tageslicht ins Innere fällt. Die Treppe und das Wohnzimmer sind durch eine Drehtür aus Holz verbunden, die eine zentrale Achse hat, die um 360 Grad gedreht werden kann. Die Küche aus Edelstahl wirkt industriell. Die Mischung von verschiedenen Materialien, die sich an den jeweiligen Raum anpassen, bereichert die gesamte Atmosphäre.

The stairway, which is adjacent to the living room, leads to the bedrooms and the bathroom. The transparent risers allow light to filter through.

L'escalier, attenant au salon, mène aux chambres à coucher et à la salle de bains.

Die Treppe neben dem Wohnzimmer führt zu den Schlafzimmern und zum Bad. Durch die transparenten Stufen fällt ebenfalls Licht.

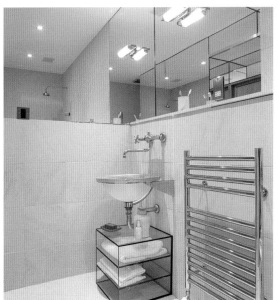

The rotating door in the kitchen - inspired by garage doors - creates a separation between the kitchen from the dining room.

La porte pivotante de la cuisine, inspirée des portes de garages, permet de séparer la cuisine de la salle à manger.

Mithilfe der Drehtür der Küche, die einer Garagentür gleicht, kann man die Küche vom Speisezimmer abtrennen.

Penthouse on Gran Via
Attique sur la Gran Via
Dachwohnung in Gran Via

Barcelona, Spain

The most distinctive feature of this penthouse apartment is its unique location, as well as the functional layout required by its owners. The initial goal was to transform two sizeable apartments into one single space capable of housing three well-defined areas that would each possess a distinct personality and function. This was dubbed a 'three-in-one conversion' by the team of architects commissioned to carry out the renovation. This flexible living space in a historical building was designed for a family with two children and so responds to their everyday needs. Each member of the family has at his or her disposal a complete living area, designed as a small apartment within the overall container of the house. Thus, the spaces are independent from one another, each with a kitchen, bathroom, and independent living room, which simultaneously serve as rooms integrated into the overall space.

Ce qui caractérise cet attique c'est la singularité du lieu et le programme fonctionnel exigé par le client. Ce projet a pour but initial, la transformation de deux appartements anciens en un espace unique, accueillant trois zones bien définies avec leur entité, personnalité et fonctionnalité respectives. Cette réhabilitation a été baptisée par l'équipe d'architectes du nom de « trois en un ». L'habitation polyvalente, située dans une propriété de campagne de grande valeur historique et conçue pour une famille de trois enfants, est planifiée pour satisfaire les besoins quotidiens. Chacun des membres de la famille dispose d'une zone d'habitation complète, conçue à l'instar d'un petit appartement complet au sein d'un container général. Chaque espace est ainsi autonome, avec cuisine, salle de bains et salon indépendants, qui sont à leur tour des pièces intégrées au grand espace de l'étage central.

Was diese Dachwohnung so einzigartig macht, ist ihre Lage und die funktionelle Aufteilung, die sich der Kunde wünschte. Hauptziel war es, aus zwei herrschaftlichen Wohnungen eine einzige Umgebung zu machen, in der sich drei deutlich definierte Bereiche befinden, die eine eigene Einheit bilden und eine eigene Persönlichkeit und Funktion haben. Diese Umformung wurde von dem beauftragten Architektenteam als „drei in einem" getauft. Die vielseitige Wohnung, die sich in einem historisch wertvollen Gebäude befindet und für eine Familie mit zwei Kindern geplant wurde, erfüllt die Anforderungen des täglichen Lebens. Jedes Familienmitglied verfügt über einen eigenen, selbstständigen Bereich, der als kleine Wohnung in einer großen Wohnumgebung angelegt ist. So verfügt jeder Bereich über eine eigene Küche, Bad und Wohnzimmer, die gleichzeitig Räume der großen, zentralen Wohnung sind.

These spaces are not separated from one another, as they were designed to form a single unit. The armchairs in the living room are set off by a group of modern paintings.

Les espaces semblent absents de limites séparatrices et faire partie d'une seule unité. Au-dessus des fauteuils du salon, certains tableaux modernes sont mis en valeur.

Die Räume scheinen keine Begrenzungen zu haben und werden wie eine einzige Einheit behandelt. Über den Sesseln im Wohnzimmer hängen einige modernistische Bilder.

Functional solutions were sought for the bedrooms; these include mobile closets that make the spaces more flexible.

Dans la chambre, des solutions fonctionnelles ont été privilégiées, à l'instar d'armoires mobiles qui dotent l'espace d'une grande flexibilité.

Im Schlafzimmer entschied man sich für funktionelle Lösungen wie mobile Schränke, die den Raum sehr flexibel machen.

Residence on Elsie Street
Résidence dans Elsie Street
Haus in Elsie Street

San Francisco, USA

The owners of this private residence, located on a terraced urban lot, wanted a New York-style loft, with a private garden. Space and light were given precedence in the design. The main living area contains a living room, kitchen/dining room, and suite, and it is oriented to receive plenty of natural light. The lower level holds a studio and guest bedroom that extends over the garage. The main bedroom floats on a bright volume and offers the visitor an unusual view of the rest of the house, making it appear larger than it actually is. The house was designed in keeping with strict municipal regulations and with the character of the neighborhood. One of the most interesting features in the living room is the fireplace, whose straight, simple lines stretch upward to the ceiling and accentuate the verticality of the layout, through an unusual reiterative interplay of horizontal and vertical planes.

Les propriétaires de cette résidence privée, située sur un terrain urbain à la topographie échelonnée, voulaient un loft dans le style new-yorkays, doté d'un jardin privatif. Espace et lumière sont les lignes directrices du design. La zone d'habitation principale, comprenant un salon, une cuisine/salle à manger et une suite, est orientée pour recevoir une grande quantité de lumière. Le niveau inférieur abrite un studio doté d'une chambre d'amis installée au-dessus du garage. La chambre à coucher principale flotte au sein d'un volume lumineux et diaphane, doté d'une étrange perspective qui rehausse l'ampleur de l'espace. La maison a été conçue en respectant les normes communales strictes, pour ne pas dénaturer le quartier. Dans le salon, on est frappé par la structure rectiligne et sobre de la cheminée qui s'élève vers le plafond, accentuant la verticalité de la distribution intérieure, dans un jeu récurrent et insolite de plans horizontaux et verticaux.

Die Besitzer dieses Privathauses auf einem stufenförmigen Grundstück wünschten sich ein Loft im Stile New Yorks mit einem privaten Garten. Der Hauptwohnbereich, in dem ein Wohnzimmer, eine Essküche und Suite liegen, ist so ausgerichtet, dass sehr viel Tageslicht einfällt. Auf der unteren Ebene liegt ein kleines Studio mit Gästezimmer, das sich über der Garage befindet. Das Hauptschlafzimmer schwebt in einem hellen und transparenten Element mit einer Perspektive, die die Größe des Raums unterstreicht. Bei der Gestaltung des Hauses wurden die örtlichen Bauvorschriften berücksichtigt und es wurde ebenfalls darauf geachtet, dass sich das Haus in das umgebende Viertel gut einfügt. Im Wohnzimmer dominiert der Kamin mit seiner geraden Linienführung. Er reicht bis zu der hohen Decke und unterstreicht die Vertikalität der Raumaufteilung mit ihrem interessanten und sich wiederholendem Spiel mit horizontalen und vertikalen Flächen.

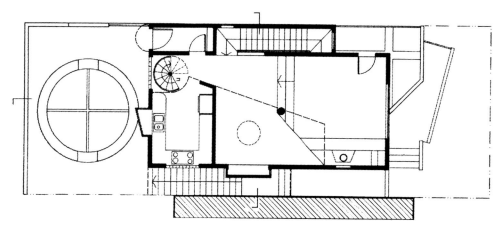

› Lower floor   Etage inférieur   Erdgeschoss

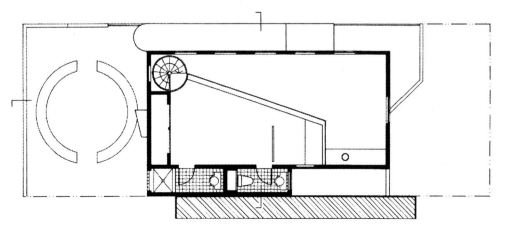

› Upper floor   Etage supérieur   Obergeschoss

The materials chosen for the bathroom play with the versatile colors found throughout the rest of the apartment.

Le choix des matériaux de la salle de bains joue avec la gamme chromatique changeante qui définit le reste de l'habitation.

Auch bei den im Bad verwendeten Materialien wiederholt sich das Spiel mit den Farben, das die ganze Wohnung prägt.

Apartment in Notting Hill
Appartement à Notting Hill
Appartement in Notting Hill

London, UK

Alterations to this apartment involved removing most of the existing partitions, although some original elements were preserved such as the fireplaces, wooden structures, and ceiling moldings. The idea of the new program was to set up a permanent dialog between the old and the new. Practically all the furniture was designed to solve specific problems and to compatibilize the twofold use of the interior as dwelling and office space. Thanks to the special lighting installation, objects seem to float in the air, leading to a light, versatile interior that emphasizes empty space. One of the main rooms serves a double purpose, since during the day it functions as a study. The closets, filing cabinets, and work tables were specially designed to go unnoticed during non-working hours.

Suite à la réhabilitation de cette habitation, la plupart des cloisons existantes ont disparu, mais certains détails d'origine ont été respectés, à l'instar des cheminées, des structures de bois ou des moulures aux plafonds. L'idée du nouveau programme est d'instaurer un dialogue permanent entre l'ancien et le nouveau. Presque tout le mobilier a été conçu pour résoudre les problèmes spécifiques et réunir dans un même espace habitation et bureau. L'éclairage spécial fait que les objets semblent flotter dans l'atmosphère, créant un intérieur léger et polyvalent qui met l'accent sur le vide. Une des pièces principales fait double emploi, car pendant la journée elle fonctionne comme studio. Les armoires, fichiers et bureaux ont été spécialement conçus pour passer inaperçus en dehors des heures de bureau.

Bei der Renovierung dieser Wohnung wurden zunächst alle existierenden Raumteilungen entfernt, obwohl einige der Originalelemente wie die Kamine, die Holzstrukturen und das Deckengesims erhalten blieben. Durch die Neugestaltung entstand ein ständiger Dialog zwischen dem Neuen und dem Alten. Fast alle Möbel wurden speziell dazu entworfen, bestimmte Probleme zu lösen und die Nutzung des gleichen Raums als Wohnraum und Büro zu ermöglichen. Es wurde eine besondere Beleuchtung installiert, die den Effekt hat, dass die Objekte im Raum zu schweben scheinen und es entstanden vielseitige und leichte Räume, in denen die Leere dominiert. Eines der großen Schlafzimmer kann doppelt genutzt werden, tagsüber nämlich dient es als Studio. Die Schränke, Aktenschränke und Arbeitstische wurden so gestaltet, dass man sie als solche nicht erkennt, solange dort nicht gearbeitet wird.

The furniture, designed specifically for this apartment by Torsten Neeland, combines with some of the original elements, such as the fireplace.

Le mobilier, de Torsten Neeland, a été spécialement conçu pour cet appartement, en harmonie avec certains des détails originaux comme la cheminée.

Das Mobiliar wurde speziell für diese Wohnung von Torsten Neeland entworfen und mit einigen der bereits existierenden Elementen, wie dem Kamin kombiniert.

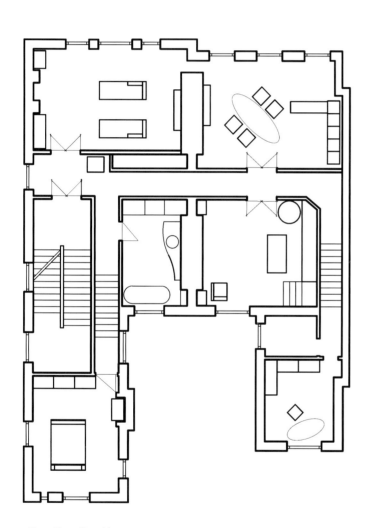

› Plan Plan Grundriss

Zartoshty Loft
Loft Zartoshty
Loft Zartoshty

Boston, USA

Located on the top floor of a loft building, this apartment was reconverted into an open-plan space without too many pretensions. Following the owner's instructions, the architect designed a single environment marked by the presence of the living and dining areas, and of an entirely open kitchen that enhances the specified visual continuity. One of its sides stretches alongside the dining area to serve as a bar, for having breakfast, a snack or a drink. The prevailing formal simplicity is the fruit of the perfect combination of straight lines. A stairway, concealed behind a tall closet, leads up to the attic, which accommodates the master bedroom, the bathroom, and the study. A limited range of materials was used to blur the differences between the rooms. The doors and flooring are of dark, matt-finished walnut, in contrast with the sheen of the other surfaces.

Situé au dernier étage d'un édifice de lofts, cet appartement a été reconverti en un espace ouvert sans grandes prétentions. Selon les instructions du propriétaire, l'architecte a conçu une atmosphère unique, définie par le salon et la salle à manger et par une cuisine entièrement ouverte soulignant ainsi la continuité visuelle requise. Un des murs latéraux s'étend devant la salle à manger pour former un bar où prendre le déjeuner, un apéritif ou un encas. L'ensemble revêt une grande simplicité formelle grâce à la combinaison parfaite de ses lignes droites. Un escalier, caché derrière une grande armoire, conduit vers les combles, où se trouvent la chambre à coucher principale, la salle de bains et le studio. La palette limitée de matériaux vise à effacer la différence entre les espaces de vie. Les portes et les sols sont en noyer foncé doté d'un fini mat qui contraste avec le verni du reste des superficies.

Dieses Loft im Obergeschoss eines Fabrikgebäudes wurde zu einer offenen und relativ bescheidenen Wohnung umgebaut. Der Eigentümer wünschte sich einen einzigen Raum, in dem es ein Wohnzimmer, ein Esszimmer und eine völlig offene Küche gibt, so dass die visuelle Kontinuität bestehen bleibt. Eine der Küchenwände reicht bis vorne an das Esszimmer, wo sich eine Bar für das Frühstück, einen Aperitif oder Imbiss befindet. Der vorherrschende Eindruck von Schlichtheit entsteht aufgrund der perfekt kombinierten, geraden Linien. Eine hinter einem hohen Schrank verborgene Treppe führt in eine Mansarde, in der sich das Schlafzimmer, das Bad und das Atelier befinden. Es wurden nur wenig verschiedene Materialien eingesetzt, mit denen man die Unterschiedlichkeit der Räume unterstrich. Die Türen und der Boden sind aus Nussbaum mit matter Oberfläche, die einen Kontrast zu den übrigen polierten Flächen bildet.

› First floor Premier étage Erstes Obergeschoss

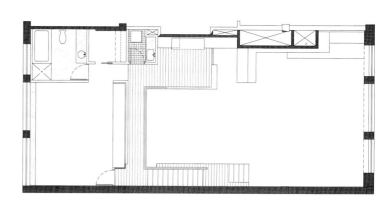

› Mezzanine Mezzanine Mezanine

The living area is presided over by the simple, entirely white fireplace, which creates a relaxed atmosphere.

Dans le salon, la cheminée, totalement blanche et aux lignes simples, se détache du reste et procure une ambiance décontractée et paisible.

Im Wohnzimmer hebt sich die völlig weiße Struktur des Kamins mit ihren einfachen Linien ab. Die Atmosphäre ist einladend und freundlich.

Boesky Loft
Loft Boesky
Loft Boesky

New York, USA

The art dealer who purchased this loft required a space in which to exhibit her private art collection. The dwelling was required to meet the owner's needs and provide functional scope for various activities, while readily accommodating a large variety of furniture on the perimeter. In the living room, shelves were designed to exhibit many of the photographs and drawings from her collection. The ceiling contains skylights that enhance the illumination of specific points in the apartment or pinpointparticular objets d'art. The division into public and private space coincides with the division into floors: the floor below accommodates the living and dining rooms, a study, and an exhibition gallery, while the one above contains another study, the master bedroom, the bathroom, and an outside terrace that allows natural light to penetrate.

La propriétaire de ce loft, une marchande d'art, cherchait un espace adéquat pour exposer sa collection d'art privé. L'habitation devait à la fois répondre à ses besoins personnels et apporter des solutions fonctionnelles à la répartition des diverses activités et en même temps accueillir un mobilier très varié sur tout le périmètre. Dans le salon, des étagères ont été conçues pour abriter une multitude de photographies et de dessins issus du fond artistique. Des velux, installés au plafond, accentuent l'éclairage de certaines zones concrètes ou d'objets d'art particuliers. La division des espaces publics et privés coïncide avec celle des étages : le premier étage abrite le salon, la salle à manger, un bureau et une galerie d'exposition. L'étage supérieur dispose d'un autre studio, avec une chambre à coucher principale, une salle de bains et une terrasse extérieure qui permet à la lumière d'inonder l'espace.

Ein Kunsthändler hatte dieses Loft erworben und wünschte sich eine Umgebung, die zur Ausstellung seiner privaten Kunstsammlung geeignet sei. Außerdem musste Platz für eine Vielzahl an Möbeln geschaffen werden. Diese Anforderungen mussten bei der Planung erfüllt werden und man suchte funktionelle Lösungen für die Verteilung der verschiedenen Aktivitäten. Im Wohnzimmer brachte man ein Regal an, in dem die vielen Fotos und Zeichnungen aus der Sammlung Platz finden. In die Decke wurden Dachfenster eingebaut, durch die Licht auf konkrete Punkte und bestimmte Kunstwerke fällt. Die Aufteilung der von allen genutzten und privateren Räume entspricht der Aufteilung der Stockwerke. Im Untergeschoss liegen das Wohnzimmer, das Esszimmer, ein Atelier und die Austellungsgalerie, im Obergeschoss ein weiteres Atelier, das Hauptschlafzimmer, das Bad und eine Außenterrasse, von der Licht in die Räume fällt.

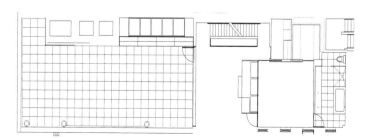

› First floor Premier étage Erstes Obergeschoss

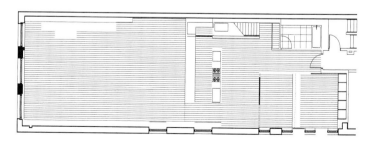

› Second floor Deuxième étage Zweites Obergeschoss

One of the key decisions consisted of using translucent mobile partitions to guarantee the flow of light inside the apartment

Une des décisions majeures est l'emploi de divisions amovibles et translucides pour garantir le flux de lumière vers les espaces.

Eine wichtige Entscheidung war der Einsatz von mobilen, lichtdurchlässigen Raumteilern, durch die das Licht in die Räume strömt.

The terrace is ideal for open-air meals. The shower at one end provides a refreshing sequel to sunbathing.

La terrasse permet d'organiser des repas en plein air. Une douche, installée à l'une de ses extrémités, permet de se rafraîchir après avoir pris un bain de soleil.

Die Terrasse wird als Esszimmer im Freien benutzt. An einem Ende der Terrasse befindet sich eine Dusche, in der man sich nach dem Sonnenbad erfrischen kann.

Barge & Murphy Loft
Loft Barge & Murphy
Loft Barge & Murphy

London, UK

The architects took advantage of the scope provided by this Victorian building to convert its top floor into a loft. Having studied the parameters of the 2,153-sq.-ft surface area, they rearranged the space and converted it into a loft divided into two parallel blocks. The main focus of the refurbishment the roof. In one of the wings, seven windows were opened to the south, but with views to the east and west. In the other, three fanlights frame small portions of sky. The set of pavilions was connected directly to the departments located immediately below, where the Barge & Murphy loft is situated. Each of them features a transparent, crystalline ceiling through which natural light can penetrate into the interior.

Les architectes ont tiré profit des avantages offerts par la structure originale, située dans une construction victorienne, pour transformer la partie supérieure en attique. Après avoir étudié les paramètres des 200 m² de superficie, ils ont redistribué l'espace et l'ont converti en un loft organisé autour de deux blocs parallèles. L'ampleur de la réhabilitation concerne surtout la construction de la toiture. Sept grandes verrières percent une des ailes qui s'ouvre ainsi vers le sud offrant des vues sur l'est et l'ouest. L'autre aile est perforée de trois velux qui encadrent des petits morceaux de ciel. L'ensemble des pavillons est relié directement aux départements situés immédiatement au-dessous, emplacement exact du loft Barge & Murphy. Chacun des espaces intérieurs est recouvert d'une toiture cristalline et transparente permettant à la lumière de pénétrer partout.

Dieses Loft liegt in einem viktorianischen Haus, dessen Originalstruktur die Architekten nutzten, um den oberen Bereich zu einer Dachwohnung umzubauen. Nachdem man die Verteilung der Wände auf der 200 m² großen Fläche analysiert hatte, wurde der Raum neu verteilt und das Loft in zwei parallele Blöcke strukturiert. Der wichtigste Eingriff war die Konstruktion des Daches. In einem der Flügel öffnen sich sieben große Fenster nach Süden, von denen man einen Ausblick nach Osten und nach Westen hat. In dem anderen gibt es Dachfenster, durch die man kleine Stücke des Himmels sieht. Die Pavillongruppe wurde direkt mit den Wohnungen verbunden, die direkt darunter liegen. Dort befindet sich auch das Loft Barge & Murphy. In jeder Wohnung gibt es ein transparentes Glasdach, durch das Licht ins Innere fällt.

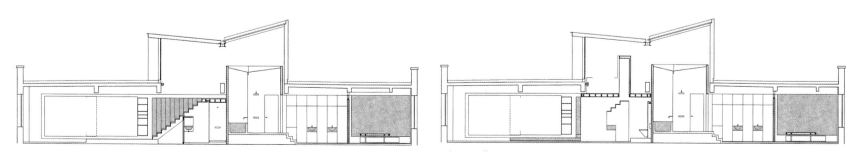

› Sections Sections Schnitte

The purity of materials and simplicity of forms in the bathroom create a serene atmosphere conducive to relaxation.

La pureté des matériaux et la simplicité des formes de la salle de bains parviennent à créer une atmosphère paisible qui invite à la détente.

Die Reinheit der Materialien und die Einfachheit der Formen des Bades schaffen eine ruhige und entspannende Atmosphäre.

Ian Chee Apartment

Appartement Ian Chee

Appartement Ian Chee

London, UK

The objective of this project was to convert a former garage into a luminous open-plan apartment accommodating all the conveniences associated with an apartment. The architects decided to share the available space among three rooms as well as to create an inner patio to intensify the lighting in the central area. In this way, they managed to enhance the feeling of spaciousness and establish a visual link with the exterior, while reorganizing the original floor space which was enclosed and lacking in views. The remaining rooms are on the floor above, reached by a staircase without risers whose geometrical structure stands out at the far end of the living room. Thanks to the absence of superfluous elements, light plays a predominant role.

L'objectif de ce projet était de réhabiliter un ancien garage en une habitation ouverte et lumineuse dotée des caractéristiques propres à un appartement. Les architectes décidèrent de distribuer l'espace en trois pièces et de créer un patio intérieur pour intensifier l'éclairage dans la partie centrale de l'habitation. Cela permit d'accroître la sensation d'ampleur et d'établir un lien visuel avec l'extérieur, tout en réorganisant le plan d'origine, fermé et sans vues. Les autres pièces sont distribuées à l'étage supérieur, auquel on accède par un escalier sans contre marche dont la structure géométrique se détache du fond de la salle de séjour. L'absence d'éléments superflus laisse la lumière être le protagoniste de l'espace.

Eine ehemalige Garage sollte zu einer offenen und hellen Wohnung umgebaut werden, die alles enthält, was man zum komfortablen Wohnen benötigt. Die Architekten unterteilten den vorhandenen Raum in drei Zimmer und schufen einen Innenhof, durch den der mittlere Teil der Wohnung heller wird. So entstand das Gefühl von Weite sowie eine visuelle Verbindung nach außen, während gleichzeitig der originale Grundriss, der geschlossen war und keine Aussicht nach außen hatte, neu gestaltet wurde. Die übrigen Räume befinden sich auf der oberen Etage, zu der man über eine Treppe ohne Setzstufen gelangt. Die geometrische Struktur dieser Treppe fällt im Hintergrund des Wohnzimmers ins Auge. Um das Licht zum Hauptdarsteller zu machen, verzichtete man auf jede Art von überflüssigen Elementen.

The staircase without risers enhances the industrial nature of this former garage.

L'escalier sans contremarche souligne le caractère industriel de cet ancien garage.

Die Treppe ohne Setzstufen unterstreicht die industrielle Atmosphäre in dieser ehemaligen Garage.

A central skylight solves the problem of inadequate illumination of the original structure.

Un velux central résout le problème de luminosité lié à la structure initiale.

Ein zentrales Dachfenster erhellt diesen einst sehr dunklen Raum.

Ryan Apartment
Appartement Ryan
Appartement Ryan

Sydney, Australia

The company that renovated this old-fashioned apartment dating from the 1960s sought better spatial distribution and modern design in keeping with contemporary tastes. With these aims in mind, they eliminated most of the walls to provide a new layout that unified the various parts of the home. The living-room walls are now sliding glass doors that, together with the transparent terrace parapet, allow the occupants to enjoy splendid views of Bondi beach. White predominates throughout, providing a neutral counterpoint to the extraordinary panoramic views and the designer furniture. PTW Architects' philosophy is to analyze each of their assigned architectural tasks in order to offer detailed design solutions.

L'entreprise chargée de la restauration de cet appartement désuet des années soixante a cherché à améliorer la distribution spatiale selon un design plus moderne, plus proche de l'époque actuelle. Pour y parvenir, la majeure partie des murs a été éliminée pour créer une nouvelle distribution unifiant les différentes zones de l'habitation. Dans le salon, les murs sont constitués de portes coulissantes de verre, qui, avec la transparence du parapet de la terrasse, offrent à ses habitants la possibilité de jouir de l'intérieur des splendides vues sur la plage Bondi. Le blanc, couleur qui domine toutes les pièces à vivre de la maison, offre un contraste neutre face aux vues panoramiques extraordinaires et au mobilier design qui met en scène l'espace. L'optique professionnelle du bureau PTW Architects se base sur l'analyse de chacune des taches architecturales respectives afin d'apporter des concepts de solutions détaillés.

Das Unternehmen, das dieses ältere Appartement aus den Sechzigerjahren renovierte, suchte eine bessere Verteilung der Räume und ein modernes, zeitgenössisches Design. Dazu wurde der größte Teil der Wände entfernt und der Raum neu aufgeteilt. Die verschiedenen Wohnbereiche wurden vereinheitlicht. Im Wohnzimmer bestehen die Wände aus gläsernen Schiebetüren, ebenso transparent ist die Brüstung der Terrasse, so dass die Bewohner einen wundervollen Blick auf den Strand Bondi haben. Die Farbe Weiß spielt die Hauptrolle in allen Räumen und bildet einen neutralen Kontrapunkt zu dem außerordentlich schönen Panoramablick und den edlen Möbeln, die die Räumlichkeiten prägen. Die Arbeitsweise von PTW Architects basiert auf einer Analyse jeder einzelnen architektonischen Aufgabe, um Gestaltungslösungen in allen Einzelheiten bieten zu können.

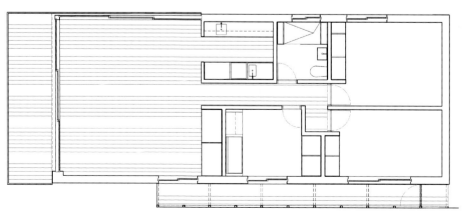

› Plan Plan Grundriss

The materials were chosen to create an overall feeling of neutrality and delicacy.

Les matériaux sélectionnés confèrent à l'ensemble une allure neutre et peaufinée.

Die gewählten Materialien lassen die Umgebung neutral und sehr rein wirken.

San Francisco, USA

21st Street

The remodeling of this Victorian-style apartment explores the effects of transparency in both the literal and figurative senses. Glazed walls and partitions offer a wide variety of possible readings of space at different times of the day. The glass box that accommodates the bathroom constitutes the perfect division between the privacy inherent to this space and the communal nature of the kitchen. Furthermore, during the day light penetrates the bathroom through the south-facing kitchen, thereby creating a bright, warm atmosphere. At night, this translucent volume shines green, with the help of fluorescent gels. The architect managed to integrate and reinterpret the Victorian elements by using steel details in her endeavor to find a point of encounter between the beauty of the original architecture and the purity of the contemporary elements, further highlighted by the abstract artworks and carefully chosen pieces of furniture.

La restructuration de cette habitation de style victorien explore les effets de la transparence au sens littéral et figuré. Murs et cloisons de verre permettent diverses lectures de l'espace en fonction de l'heure du jour. La boîte de verre, qui héberge la salle de bains, incarne la division parfaite entre l'intimité inhérente à cet espace et l'espace commun naturel de la cuisine. En outre, pendant la journée la lumière baigne cet espace par le biais de la cuisine, orientée vers le sud, imprégnant l'atmosphère de chaleur et luminosité. La nuit, le volume transparent resplendit de couleur verte, grâce aux gels fluorescents. L'architecture a su intégrer les éléments victoriens et les réinterpréter en utilisant des détails en acier. Il fallait créer un point de rencontre entre la beauté de l'architecture d'origine et la pureté des éléments contemporains par le biais des œuvres d'art abstrait et du mobilier concret.

Beim Umbau dieses Wohnhauses im viktorianischen Stil wurde auf die Wirkung der Transparenz im wörtlichen und im übertragenen Sinne gesetzt. Die verglasten Wände lassen den Raum zu den verschiedenen Tageszeiten immer wieder anders wirken. Der Glaskasten, in dem sich das Bad befindet, stellt eine perfekte Abtrennung zwischen der Privatsphäre des Bades und dem gemeinschaftlichen Charakter der Küche dar. Außerdem fällt tagsüber das Licht durch die Küche nach Süden bis zu diesem Punkt, was die Atmosphäre warm und hell macht. Nachts leuchtet diese lichtdurchlässige Form mit Hilfe von fluoreszierendem Gel grün. Die Architektin integrierte geschickt die viktorianischen Elemente und interpretierte sie durch den Gebrauch von Einzelheiten aus Stahl neu. Es sollte ein Aufeinandertreffen zwischen der Schönheit der Originalarchitektur und der Reinheit der zeitgenössischen Elemente stattfinden.

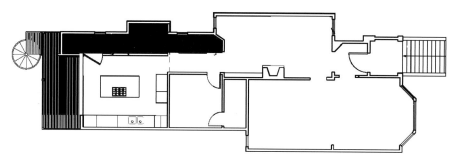

› Plan Plan Grundriss

The kitchen, which opens on to the terrace, ensures the penetration of natural light, which filters through transparent surfaces and reflects off polished ones.

La cuisine, ouverte sur la terrasse, préserve à tout moment l'entrée de la lumière naturelle, filtrée à l'intérieur grâce aux surfaces transparentes et vernies.

In die zur Terrasse offene Küche fällt den ganzen Tag über Tageslicht, das durch transparente und polierte Flächen ins Innere gefiltert wird.

The terrace adjoining the bedroom provides light and transparency, offset by the starkness of the materials.

La terrasse attenante à la chambre à coucher assure un espace diaphane et transparent dominé par la sobriété des matériaux.

Die Terrasse am Schlafzimmer lässt diesen Raum transparent und offen wirken. Die verwendeten Materialien sind sehr schlicht.

Loft in Buenos Aires
Loft à Buenos Aires
Loft in Buenos Aires

Buenos Aires, Argentina

This loft, located in one of the city's old warehouses, is characterized by its contemporary lines and a measured selection of furniture and objects. The space adopts a simple L-shape in which public and private areas are marked off by translucent fabric. Contrast is one of the prevailing features of this project and endows the apartment with great versatility. White and dark wood defines the color scheme while contemporary objects are combined with furniture from the 1940s and 1950s. Beneath the stairway, the kitchen is separated from the living room by a laminated mahogany partition. The steel columns, the ceiling vault, and the large windows constantly recall the original purpose of the loft. The verticality of the curtains, which conceal the bedroom, emphasizes the height of the ceiling, and their translucency endows the bedroom with a light, intimate quality.

Ce loft, situé dans d'anciens entrepôts de la ville, se définit par ses lignes contemporaines et un choix judicieux de meubles et objets. La distribution de l'espace suit un plan simple en forme de L. Les pièces privées et publiques sont délimitées par une toile translucide qui les sépare. Le contraste est une des idées récurrentes de ce projet qu'il imprègne ainsi d'une grande polyvalence. L'alternance de bois blanc et foncé définit la gamme chromatique de l'espace et les objets contemporains se mêlent au mobilier de 1940 et 1950. Située sous l'escalier, la cuisine est séparée du salon par une cloison laminée en bois d'acajou. Les colonnes en acier, la voûte du toit et les grandes fenêtres rappellent constamment le concept initial du loft. La verticalité des rideaux, qui masquent la chambre à coucher, accentuent la hauteur du toit et leur transparence ajoute une note d'intimité et de légèreté à la chambre à coucher.

Dieses Loft liegt in einem ehemaligen Kaufhaus. Es zeichnet sich durch die zeitgenössischen Linien und die maßvolle Auswahl von Möbeln und Objekten aus. Die Raumaufteilung beruht auf einer einfachen L-Form, wobei die von allen genutzten Bereiche von den privateren Räumen durch einen lichtdurchlässigen Stoff abgetrennt sind. Weißes und dunkles Holz bilden die Farbskala der Räume, und zeitgenössische Objekte werden mit Möbeln aus den Jahren zwischen 1940 und 1950 kombiniert. Unter der Treppe ist die Küche vom Wohnzimmer durch eine mit Mahagoni beschichtete Trennwand abgetrennt. Die Stahlsäulen, das Gewölbe und die großen Fenster erinnern ständig daran, was sich vorher hier befand. Die vertikalen Gardinen verbergen das Schlafzimmer und betonen die Höhe der Decke. Sie sind lichtdurchlässig und machen die Atmosphäre im Schlafzimmer intim und leicht.

The column standing in the middle of the living room rationalizes the layout and preserves the original identity of the loft.

La colonne située au centre du salon rationalise la distribution des éléments et préserve l'identité originale du loft.

Die Säule in der Mitte des Wohnzimmers ist der Ausgangspunkt für die Verteilung der Elemente und gleichzeitig das Stück, das die ursprüngliche Identität dieses Lofts erhält.

Some pieces of classical furniture share space with contemporary designs, thereby setting up an attractive contrast.

Certaines pièces de mobilier classique partagent l'espace avec des dessins contemporains, créant un contraste particulier.

Durch die Kombination von klassischen Möbeln mit zeitgenössischem Design entstand ein interessanter Gegensatz.

A curtain hanging beside the bed accentuates the verticality of the room and further enhances the considerable height of the ceilings.

Un rideau suspendu à côté du lit accentue la verticalité de la pièce et souligne la hauteur considérable des toits.

Am Bett hängt eine Gardine, die die Vertikalität und Höhe des Raumes betont.

Balmoral House
Maison Balmoral
Haus Balmoral

Sydney, Australia

The building containing this two-floor apartment has undergone numerous alterations since its construction in the 1930s. The most recent refurbishment involved enlarging some of the spaces, changing some of the finishes, redesigning the entrance, and landscaping the immediate surroundings. The front porch arcade was rebuilt to recover a sunny space that opens toward the garden through folding doors, thereby establishing a close relationship with the exterior. Inside, the partitions were removed to make the living and dining rooms more spacious. Since privacy was not essential, it was decided to set both areas in the same rectangular space, where domestic functions are hidden behind the vertical dividers embellished with artworks belonging to the client.

La maison qui accueille cette habitation de deux étages, datant des années trente, a subit de multiples réformes. La dernière en date a permis d'agrandir quelques espaces, de modifier les finitions, de redessiner l'accès et de remodeler le paysage autour de la maison. L'arcade du porche avant a été reconstruite pour récupérer un espace isolé qui s'ouvre sur le jardin grâce à des portes à battants, établissant ainsi une étroite relation avec l'extérieur. L'intérieur, libéré de cloisons, gagne en amplitude, notamment dans le salon et la salle à manger. L'intimité n'étant pas de rigueur, les deux espaces ont été réunis en un seul volume rectangulaire où les fonctions domestiques se cachent derrière les parements verticaux qui accueillent les œuvres d'art de la cliente.

Das Gebäude, in dem sich diese zweistöckige Wohnung befindet, stammt aus den Dreißigerjahren des letzten Jahrhunderts und wurde bereits sehr oft umgebaut. Bei diesem letzten Eingriff wurden einige Räume erweitert, Oberflächenmaterialien verändert, der Zugang umgestaltet und eine Landschaft um das Haus geplant. Die Arkade der vorderen Veranda wurde rekonstruiert, um diesen sonnigen Ort, den man mit Falttüren zum Garten öffnen kann, wieder wohnlich zu machen. So entstand eine Verbindung zum Garten. Im Inneren wurden Zwischenwände herausgenommen, um das Wohn- und Esszimmer größer zu machen. Die Kunden wünschten sich nicht sehr viel Intimität, deshalb konnten beide Bereiche im gleichen, rechteckigen Raum angebracht werden, wo die häuslichen Funktionen hinter vertikalen Mauern angedeutet werden, an denen sich Kunstwerke aus dem Besitz der Kunden befinden.

A single-piece rectangular module marks the limits of the kitchen and endows it with a professional look.

Un module rectangulaire d'un seul tenant délimite la cuisine, lui octroyant ainsi une image professionnelle.

Ein rechteckiges Modul setzt die Begrenzungen der Küche fest und lässt sie professionell wirken.

The aesthetic and functional potential of this apartment is reflected in a number of details, such as partitions that do not reach the ceiling and openings that allow natural light to penetrat.

Le potentiel esthétique et fonctionnel de cette habitation se reflète dans certains détails, à l'instar des cloisons qui ne vont pas jusqu'au plafond et des ouvertures qui permettent l'accès de la lumière naturelle.

In dieser sehr ästhetischen und funktionellen Wohnung gibt es Einzelheiten wie Wände, die die Decke nicht berühren, die die Schönheit und Funktionalität noch unterstreichen.

The simple, functional space shuns complicated structures. The bathroom occupies a private corner isolated from the rest of the rooms.

Loin des complications constructives, l'espace est simple et fonctionnel. La salle de bains est lovée dans un coin intime isolé des autres pièces.

Der Raum ist einfach und funktionell, ohne bauliche Komplikationen. Das Bad befindet sich in einem intimen Winkel, abgetrennt von den übrigen Räumen.

Goldsborough Loft

Loft Goldsborough

Loft Goldsborough

London, UK

Glyn Emrys and Pascal Madoc Jones, the two partners in AEM, were perfectly aware that converting industrial space into a dwelling is not a purely aesthetic process but rather the expression of empathy with the client's attitude to life. One aspect of this complicity was the mutual base spaces, which meant, on the one hand, that the architects had to rule out dividing walls and camouflage storage space and, on the other, that the client had to combine several activities in a single space. In the case of this loft, the result is exemplary, as the color scheme of the few pieces of furniture and the modulation of to light by filters endorse the commitment not only respect the existing construction but also to enhance the underlying lyricism of this kind of space.

Glyn Emrys et Pascal Madoc Jones, les deux partenaires de AEM, ont parfaitement compris que la conversion d'un espace industriel en habitation ne peut être purement d'ordre esthétique. En effet, elle naît d'une attitude vitale déterminée par le client, exigeant que les architectes comprennent cette dualité. Un des facteurs de cette complicité entre les acteurs est l'attirance mutuelle pour les espaces dénudés, ce qui suppose, d'une part, que l'architecte évite les partitions et masque les espaces de rangement, et de l'autre, que le client sache dissimuler l'existence de plusieurs activités en un seul espace. Dans ce loft, la réponse à ce choix est exemplaire. En effet, le traitement chromatique des rares pièces de mobilier et la modulation de la lumière au travers de filtres, adhèrent parfaitement au compromis de ne pas modifier la construction existante, et, de surcroît, parviennent à déployer le lyrisme inhérent à ce type d'espaces.

Glyn Emrys und Pascal Madoc Jones von AEM verstanden perfekt, dass die Entscheidung, einen industriellen Raum in einen Wohnraum zu verwandeln, nicht nur ein rein ästhetischer Eingriff ist, sondern dass sie die Lebenseinstellung des Kunden widerspiegelt, die der Architekt verstehen muss. Einer der Faktoren, in dem sich Architekten und Kunde einig waren, war die Vorliebe für nackte, leere Räume. Das bedeutet, dass der Architekt Trennwände vermeiden und Lagerräume verbergen sollte, und dass der Kunde dazu fähig sein sollte, mehrere Aktivitäten in einem einzigen Raum zu vereinbaren. In diesem Loft wurden diese Anforderungen beispielhaft gelöst. Durch die farbliche Behandlung der wenigen Möbel und die Abstufungen des Lichtes durch Filter erreichte man es nicht nur, die existierende Konstruktion unverändert zu lassen, sondern man öffnete sich auch dem Charme, den diese Art von Räumen besitzen.

The orange-colored central module of the kitchen conforms perfectly to the prevailing industrial style.

Dans cet espace ouvert, le module central de la cuisine se détache du reste : de couleur orange, il s'intègre parfaitement au style industriel de l'ensemble.

In dem offenen Raum hebt sich das zentrale, orangefarbene Küchenmodul ab, das sich perfekt in den industriellen Stil der Wohnumgebung einfügt.

Penthouse in Barcelona
Attique à Barcelone
Dachwohnung in Barcelona

Barcelona, Spain

This building, whose L-shape embraces what was originally a sheet-metal workshop, dates from the beginning of the 20th century. Pere Cortacans was responsible for the refurbishment of the entire building, including the conversion of the workshop into a central garden. Furthermore, the architect reserved one of the top-floor dwellings for himself. This penthouse has three floors: the first corresponds to the original story; the second is a mezzanine, the result of dismantling the lower part of the ventilation chamber (the old air-conditioning system); while the third is a glazed studio that occupies part of the roof and provides access to a terrace. From the outset, it was established that the apartment was to be understood vertically. In this way, the bottom floor recovers the essence of the original construction without sacrificing the advantages of the transformation of the roof.

Cet édifice en forme de L embrasse un ancien atelier de tôle métallique du début du XXe siècle. Pere Cortacans, chargé de l'opération, a restauré tout l'immeuble y compris l'atelier réhabilité en jardin central. Par ailleurs, l'architecte s'est réservé une des habitations à l'étage supérieur. Cet espace dispose de trois niveaux : le premier correspond au niveau d'origine, le second, sous forme de combles, est né du démantèlement de la pièce d'air conditionné (système désuet de contrôle de l'air ambiant) et le troisième, un studio tout en verre, occupe une partie de la toiture de l'édifice avec un accès à la terrasse. Dès le départ, il a été convenu que l'habitation devait se comprendre à la verticale. Ceci étant, le rez-de-chaussée récupère l'essence de la construction d'origine tout en profitant des avantages issus de la réhabilitation de la toiture.

Dieses L-förmige Gebäude war Anfang des 20. Jh., eine Werkstatt für Metallbleche. Während des Eingriffs unter der Leitung von Pere Cortacans wurde das gesamte Gebäude saniert und die Werkstatt in einen zentralen Garten umgestaltet. Außerdem reservierte der Architekt eine der Wohnungen im Obergeschoss für sich selbst. In dieser Wohnung gibt es drei Ebenen, die erste entspricht dem originalen Grundriss, die zweite ist eine Mansarde, die dadurch entstand, dass man den unteren Teil der Entlüftungskammer abriss und die dritte Ebene ist ein verglastes Studio auf dem Dach des Gebäudes, von dem aus man die Terrasse betritt. Von Anfang an wurde die Wohnung vertikal aufgeteilt. So blieb im unteren Stock die Essenz der Originalstruktur erhalten, ohne dass dabei auf die Vorteile der Umgestaltung des Daches verzichtet werden musste.

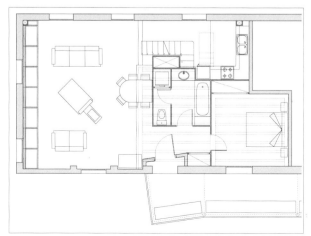

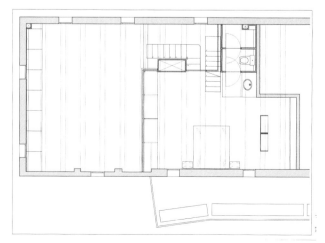

› Plan Plan Grundriss

› Mezzanine Mezzanine Mezzanine

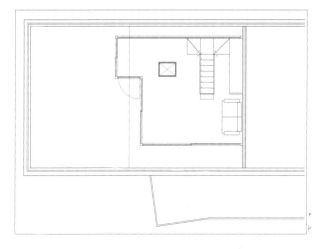

› Roof Plan   Niveau du toit   Dachplan

The element that separates the bedroom and living room consists of a shelf-bench with a small railing.

L'élément de partition entre la chambre à coucher et le salon revêt la forme d'une étagère/banc doté d'une petite balustrade.

Das Trennelement zwischen dem Schlafzimmer und dem Wohnzimmer besteht aus einer Regalbank mit einem kleinen Geländer.

Hamilton House
Maison Hamilton
Haus Hamilton

Sydney, Australia

On the site of this family's former home, the new construction establishes a close relationship with its surroundings. The imposing one-hundred-year-old tree and the opportunity to obtain matchless views meant that the building was set on the highest part of the lot. The rectangular layout contrasts with the rounded forms of the constructional elements. The architects were given a free hand when it came to designing this new setting, and devised a distribution that ensures continuity with the exterior. On the one hand, they designed large balconies from which magnificent views can be enjoyed in all directions. On the other, thanks to the curving geometry, each room establishes its own relationship with the exterior. In order to intensify the presence of light by means of huge windows and other openings on the façade.

Située sur le même terrain où fut érigée l'ancienne maison de cette famille, la nouvelle construction instaure une étroite relation avec son entourage. Un grand arbre centenaire et l'existence de vues panoramiques imprenables ont été déterminants dans l'implantation de l'édifice sur une partie élevée du terrain. Le schéma rectangulaire, où se déroule tout le programme, contraste avec les formes tout en rondeur des éléments de construction. Les architectes, totalement libres dans la réalisation de ce projet, ont conçu une distribution spatiale sous le sceau de la continuité avec l'extérieur. D'un côté, ils ont prévu de grands balcons permettant de bénéficier des vues splendides panoramiques. De l'autre, la géométrie tout en courbes a permis que chaque pièce établisse une relation individuelle et différente avec l'extérieur. De grandes verrières et diverses ouvertures dans la façade, permettent d'intensifier la présence de la lumière à l'intérieur.

Dieses Gebäude befindet sich auf dem gleichen Grundstück, auf dem das alte Familienhaus einst gebaut wurde, und es stellt eine enge Verbindung zur Umgebung her. Ein großer, hundertjähriger Baum und die Möglichkeit, einen wundervollen Blick zu haben, führten zu der Entscheidung, das Gebäude auf dem oberen Teil des Grundstücks zu errichten. Das rechteckige Schema, das auf die verschiedenen Räume angewandt wurde, steht im Gegensatz zu den abgerundeten Formen der Konstruktionselemente. Bei diesem neuen Gebäude nahmen sich die Architekten viel Freiheit und entwarfen eine Raumaufteilung, die sich nach außen fortsetzt. Einerseits schufen sie große Balkone, von denen aus man einen wundervollen Blick in alle Richtungen hat. Andererseits ermöglichten es die gekrümmten Linien, dass jeder Raum eine eigene Beziehung nach außen hat. Durch riesige Glasfenster und andere Öffnungen in der Fassade fällt reichlich Tageslicht in die Räume.

A huge window overlooking the terrace provides the living area with abundant light as well as different views of the surroundings.

Une grande verrière, donnant sur la terrasse, assure l'éclairage de la zone de séjour et offre diverses perspectives sur les alentours.

Ein großes Fenster zur Terrasse lässt viel Licht ins Wohnzimmer einfallen und man hat von verschiedenen Positionen einen interessanten Blick auf die Umgebung.

The spacious living room provides scope for a casual arrangement of decorative elements. On one side, a stairway leads to the private rooms.

L'immensité du salon laisse une grande liberté dans l'agencement des éléments décoratifs. Sur un des côtés, un escalier conduit vers les parties privées.

Das Wohnzimmer ist sehr groß, so besaß man beim Einsatz der dekorativen Elemente viel Freiraum. Auf einer Seite führt eine Treppe in die privateren Räume.

The curved nature of the load-bearing elements contributes to the architectural dynamism of the project.

La géométrie tout en courbes des éléments porteurs contribue au dynamisme architectural du projet.

Die Kurven der tragenden Elemente verstärkten die architektonische Dynamik der Umgebung.

A large module occupies the middle of the kitchen, which is predominated by stainless-steel closets.

Un grand module occupe l'espace central de la cuisine, où se détache l'acier inoxydable des armoires.

Ein großes Modul befindet sich mitten in der Küche, wo Schränke aus Edelstahl das Bild prägen.

Penthouse in Greenwich Village
Attique à Greenwich Village
Dachwohnung Greenwich Village

New York, USA

This project, located on the 14th floor of a building in New York's historic Greenwich Village, involved remodeling two apartments with a total surface area of 2,196 sq. feet, with 1,400 sq. ft of terrace at the rear and 398 sq. ft of greenhouse. The program arose from the idea of creating a space that would be the prolongation of the urban context while preserving the original structure and façade. To achieve this aim, a space was designed adjacent to the terrace. It constitutes the most industrialized element in the project and features a wide range of materials: glass, steel, aluminum, and slate. The interior follows similar lines: the architects created a mobile system of sliding doors so that the space is split into two completely differentiated zones while also blurring the borderline between the interior and the terrace.

Ce projet, situé au 14e étage d'un édifice installé dans le district historique de Greenwich Village, concerne la restructuration de deux appartements d'une superficie totale de 204 m², avec une terrasse de 130 m² à l'arrière et un jardin d'hiver de 37 m². L'implantation est née de l'idée de créer un espace qui soit la prolongation du contexte urbain, tout en conservant la structure et la façade originales. Pour cela, un espace attenant à la terrasse a été conçu, formant l'aspect davantage industriel du projet. Il a été réalisé à partir d'un large éventail de matériaux : verre, acier, aluminium et ardoise. L'intérieur est conçu de manière identique : les architectes ont créé un système mobile de portes coulissantes, de façon à ce que la zone reste divisée en deux espaces de vie complètement distincts tout en maintenant une fusion totale des limites entre l'intérieur et la terrasse.

Diese Wohnung befindet sich im 14. Stock eines Gebäudes im historischen Viertel von Greenwich Village. Zwei Wohnungen wurden zu einer einzigen mit einer Gesamtfläche von 204 m² umgebaut, zu der auch die 130 m² der hinteren Terrasse und 37 m² des Wintergartens gehören. Es sollte eine Umgebung geschaffen werden, die eine Verlängerung des städtischen Kontexts darstellt, aber die originale Struktur und Fassade beibehält. Dazu wurde ein Raum an der Terrasse entworfen, der den industrielleren Teil der Wohnung bildet und für den sehr viele unterschiedliche Materialien eingesetzt wurden, darunter Glas, Stahl, Aluminium und Schiefer. Im Inneren wird das gleiche Konzept fortgesetzt, die Architekten schufen ein mobiles System mit Schiebetüren, so dass die ganze Wohnung in zwei separate Bereiche aufgeteilt wird, in denen aber gleichzeitig die Grenzen zwischen dem Wohnungsinnerem und der Terrasse verwischen.

The space reclaimed from the terrace acts as a central meeting point from which excellent views of the urban surroundings may be enjoyed.

L'espace gagné sur la terrasse est le centre de réunion de l'habitation, où l'œil se régale des vues magnifiques sur l'environnement urbain.

Der Wintergarten dient als Treffpunkt innerhalb der Wohnung, von dem aus man einen wundervollen Blick auf die umgebende Stadtlandschaft hat.

The flooring is made of beech incrusted with ebony. Some of the materials from the terrace were also used to enhance the visual connection.

Le revêtement est en hêtre doté d'incrustations d'ébène. Dans la salle à manger, on retrouve certains des matériaux de la terrasse, ce qui exalte la continuité visuelle.

Der Bodenbelag ist aus Buche mit Einlegearbeiten aus Ebenholz. Im Speisezimmer wurden einige Materialien der Terrasse benutzt, um die visuelle Verbindung zu unterstreichen.

Shoreditch Building
Edifice Shoreditch
Gebäude Shoreditch

London, UK

A building in East London that had been abandoned for over ten years served as the basic structure for this housing project containing three luxury homes. The most outstanding feature of this spectacular project is the fact that each unit was designed individually to create a distinctive atmosphere by means of light, color and spatial organization. Special emphasis was placed on practical aspects, such as large storage areas, intelligent lighting, sound equipment and state-of-the-art technology in the bathrooms and kitchens. The lower residences occupy a single story, while the upper one is designed as an eye-catching double-height space, with a large, steel-edged glass enclosure providing a panoramic overhead view from the sitting room.

Un édifice du quartier d' East London, abandonné pendant plus de dix ans, a servi de structure de base pour développer ce projet d'habitation qui abrite désormais trois résidences de luxe. Ce qui ressort le plus de ce projet spectaculaire c'est que chacune des unités a été conçue individuellement pour atteindre dans chaque cas une atmosphère propre par le biais de la lumière, couleur et disposition de l'espace. Une attention particulière a été accordée à la conception d'un environnement pratique pour l'habitation : amplitude des zones de rangement, éclairage judicieux, installations sonores, salles de bains et cuisines, dotées de la technologie de pointe. Les pièces inférieures sont installées au rez-de-chaussée, le niveau supérieur étant un volume conçu sur deux hauteurs, très spectaculaire. Une grande coupole de verre à la structure d'acier encadre le panorama zénithal du salon.

Ein Gebäude im Viertel East London, das schon über zehn Jahre leer stand, diente als Basisstruktur für dieses Wohnhaus, in dem jetzt drei Luxuswohnungen untergebracht sind. Was dieses Gebäude sehr originell macht, ist die Tatsache, dass jede der Wohnungen individuell geplant wurde, um mithilfe von Licht, Farben und Anordnung der Räume eine eigene Atmosphäre zu schaffen. Besondere Aufmerksamkeit wurde bei der Planung darauf gelegt, die Umgebung praktisch zu gestalten. Es gibt große Lagerbereiche, intelligente Beleuchtungssysteme und Stereoanlagen, und die Bäder und Küchen sind mit der neusten Technologie ausgestattet. Die Wohnungen der unteren Stockwerke liegen auf einer Etage, während das Appartement im letzten Stockwerk zweistöckig und auffallend gestaltet ist. Eine große verglaste Wand mit Stahlprofilen dient als Rahmen für den Blick zum Himmel im Wohnzimmer.

The home is crowned by a glass enclosure that allows the occupants to enjoy a stunning panoramic view.

Une coupole de verre couronne la partie la plus élevée de l'habitation, permettant de bénéficier d'une splendide vue panoramique depuis l'intérieur.

Eine Glaswand krönt den obersten Teil der Wohnung und man hat einen wundervollen Ausblick.

The visual impact of the space is heightened by the materials and details in the interior, which is dominated by stainless steel, wood and glass.

Matériaux et détails intérieurs, présidés par l'acier inoxydable, le bois et le verre, exaltent l'amplitude de l'espace privé.

Die Materialien und Elemente im Inneren, bei denen rostfreier Stahl, Holz und Glas dominieren, unterstreichen die Wirkung der Räume.

The mixture of warm materials like the bricks on the front wall with other more polished textures conveys a sense of comfort and balance in the interior.

Le mélange de matériaux chaleureux, à l'instar de la brique du mur de façade associée à d'autres textures plus brillantes, confère à l'intérieur confort et harmonie.

Die Mischung von warmen Materialien wie die Ziegel der Vorderwand mit glatten Oberflächen vermittelt einen Eindruck von Komfort und Gleichgewicht in den Räumen.

Opaque panels provide the intimacy required by the bedroom without completely isolating it from the rest of the space.

Des panneaux accordents confèrent l'intimité nécessaire aux chambres, sans les isoler complètement de l'espace restant.

Durch undurchsichtige Paneele wird für die notwendige Intimsphäre im Schlafzimmer gesorgt, ohne dass dieses komplett von den anderen Räumen zu isoliert ist.

520 Lincoln Road

Miami, USA

The design of this apartment is the fruit of eight years' study of the efficiency, functionality, and flexibility of its interior. The space was conceived to serve as both a residence and an office. Maximum visual lightness was sought, so the apartment was provided with the minimum furniture necessary, each piece unique in terms not only of design but also of functionality. For example, the steel tables at the entrance may serve as filing cabinets, display panels, and writing desks; they may even be used as dining tables or ironing boards. A number of works by Sharon Shapiro, Lamar Briggs and Rob Calvert stand out against the white walls, their touches of color constituting the only points of reference against the neutral, barely perceivable framework of the structure. The lamps on the study tables accentuate the linear quality of the elements.

La conception de cet appartement est le fruit de huit années d'études sur l'efficacité, la fonctionnalité et la flexibilité de l'agencement intérieur. L'espace est conçu pour allier les fonctions d'habitation et de bureau. La maison recherche le maximum de légèreté visuelle, d'où la réduction du mobilier au strict nécessaire. Chaque pièce a son caractère particulier tant sur le plan du design que de la fonction. Les tables d'acier de l'entrée, par exemple, peuvent servir de meubles à classeurs, de panneaux d'exposition et de présentation et enfin de bureaux. Elles sont utilisables au gré des fonctions, à l'heure du déjeuner ou du repassage. Quelques œuvres de Sharon Shapiro, Lamar Briggs et Rob Calvert sont mises en valeur sur la toile de fond blanche des murs. Dans le cadre neutre et à peine perceptible de la structure, leurs touches de couleur sont l'unique point de référence. Posées sur la table du bureau, deux lampes exaltent le caractère linéaire des éléments.

Die Gestaltung dieses Appartements ist das Ergebnis von acht Jahren Analyse der Effizienz, der Funktionalität und der Flexibilität seiner Räume. Die Wohnung dient sowohl zum Wohnen als auch zum Arbeiten. Auf visueller Ebene suchte man Leichtigkeit, deshalb sind nur die allernötigsten Möbel vorhanden, und jedes Möbelstück ist einzigartig, nicht nur im Design, sondern auch in seiner Funktionalität. Die Stahltische am Eingang zum Beispiel können als Aktenschrank, als Ausstellungselement oder als Schreibtisch dienen; sie können sogar zum Essen und Bügeln benutzt werden. An den weißen Wänden hängen Werke von Sharon Shapiro, Lamar Briggs und Rob Calvert, die mit ihren farbigen Akzenten zum einzigen Referenzpunkt in der neutralen und fast nicht wahrnehmbaren Struktur werden. Auf den Tischen im Atelier unterstreichen zwei Lampen die Linearität der Elemente.

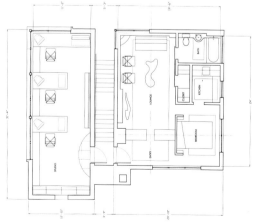

› Plan Plan Grundriss

The bathroom is partially isolated from the rest of the apartment by a glazed blue partition.

La salle de bains est pratiquement isolée du reste de l'habitation par le biais d'une superficie tout en verre bleuté.

Das Bad ist durch eine blaue, verglaste Fläche teilweise von dem übrigen Wohnraum abgetrennt.

Chrysler Factory
Usine Chrysler
Chrysler Werk

Buenos Aires, Argentina

This apartment occupies a former Chrysler factory. The interior designer, captivated by the city of Buenos Aires and inspired by the astonishing glacial landscapes of Patagonia, conceived this loft for one of the city's neoclassical buildings. From the entrance what seems to be a glacier crosses the apartment into the salon, where it becomes a dining table. The whole effect is theatrical, especially in the artificial nighttime light. The entrance platform is made of black South African marble. White, blue and gray were chosen by virtue of their resemblance to the colors of glaciers in Patagonia. The stairway leads to the floor above, which accommodates a small living room and two bedrooms, linked by a glass walkway without sacrificing their privacy. The elliptical ceiling structure was preserved and enhanced by outlining the curves in blue.

Cette habitation occupe une ancienne usine Chrysler. La décoratrice d'intérieur, captivée par la ville de Buenos Aires et sous l'inspiration des paysages glaciaires spectaculaires de la Patagonie, a conçu ce loft situé dans un des édifices néoclassiques de la ville. Depuis l'entrée, ce qui ressemble à un glacier, traverse l'habitation et parvient jusqu'au salon où il se transforme en table de repas. L'ensemble produit un effet théâtral, notamment la nuit, lorsqu'il s'éclaire artificiellement. La plate-forme d'entrée est construite en marbre noir d'Afrique du Sud. Quant aux couleurs, elles se déclinent dans une gamme de blanc, bleu et gris, à l'image des glaciers de la Patagonie. L'escalier conduit vers le niveau supérieur, où se trouvent un petit salon et deux chambres à coucher qui sont reliées par une passerelle en verre sans pour autant perdre leur caractère privé. La forme elliptique de la structure du toit a été conservée et accentuée profilant les courbes en bleu.

Diese Wohnung befindet sich in einem ehemaligen Werk von Chrysler. Die Innenarchitektin war von der Stadt Buenos Aires und von den unglaublichen Eislandschaften in Patagonien fasziniert und inspiriert, was sich auf die Planung dieses Lofts in einem neoklassischen Gebäude in der Stadt auswirkte. Am Eingang hat man den Eindruck, dass ein Gletscher die Wohnung durchquert und bis ins Wohnzimmer reicht und dort zum Esstisch wird. Das Ganze wirkt sehr theatralisch, besonders bei Nacht, wenn es künstlich beleuchtet wird. Die Plattform am Eingang ist aus schwarzem, südafrikanischem Marmor. Die verwendeten Farben sind Weiß, Blau und Grau. Eine Treppe führt nach oben, wo sich ein kleines Wohnzimmer und zwei Schlafzimmer befinden, die über einen Laufsteg aus Glas verbunden sind, aber trotzdem ihre Privatsphäre wahren. Die elliptische Form der Dachstruktur wurde erhalten und verstärkt, indem die Krümmungen blau betont wurden.

A large blue granite platform leads down into the living room, dining room, and kitchen, which are totally integrated.

Une grande plate-forme de granit bleu descend vers le salon, la salle à manger et la cuisine qui semblent totalement intégrés.

Eine große Plattform aus grauem Granit führt nach unten ins Wohnzimmer, ins Esszimmer und in die Küche, die ineinander völlig integriert sind.

The kitchen, bedrooms and other rooms are dominated by blues, grays, and whites, in order to evoke glaciers.

Que ce soit dans la cuisine, les chambres à coucher et les autres pièces, les tons bleu, gris et blanc dominent pour s'assimiler aux glaciers.

Sowohl in der Küche als auch in den Schlafzimmern und den übrigen Räumen herrschen die Farben Blau, Grau und Weiß vor, die an Gletscher erinnern.

Apartment in Miami
Appartement à Miami
Appartement in Miami

Miami, USA

The result of this project could not possibly be surpassed: space has been exploited to the maximum and solid materials like concrete have been used in accordance with contemporary criteria. The interior arrangement reflects rationalization in the use of each space. The public areas share the same open space, occasionally fragmented by an architectural element: the dining and living rooms, while sharing the same central space, are separated by a solid, imposing structure that keeps them isolated from each other. The television and audio visual equipment in one of the corners seem to constitute an extension of the living room. The uniform flooring and walls contrast with the remainder of the finishes, which are far more varied.

Ce projet ne pouvait être mieux réussi. En effet, les conditions spatiales ont été optimisées pour utiliser à bon escient les matériaux massifs comme le béton, selon des critères architecturaux contemporains. La distribution intérieure présente une rationalisation de l'emploi de chaque espace. Les zones publiques partagent le même espace ouvert, parfois fracturé par un élément architectural : la salle à manger et le salon, tout en partageant le même espace central, sont séparés par une structure massive et contondante qui permet de les différencier. Dans un angle, sorte d'extension du salon, l'espace ainsi délimité accueille la télévision et les équipements d'audio et de vidéo. L'uniformité du carrelage et des murs contraste avec le reste des finitions, beaucoup plus variées et polyvalentes.

Diese Wohnung wurde meisterhaft umgestaltet. Man wusste, das Beste aus dem vorhandenen Raum zu machen und setzte feste Materialien wie Beton perfekt ein, wobei moderne Kriterien als Grundlage dienten. Durch die innere Aufteilung wurde die Nutzungsweise jedes Bereiches rationell gestaltet. Die von allen genutzten Bereiche befinden sich im gleichen offenen Raum, der manchmal durch ein architektonisches Element unterbrochen wird. Das Speisezimmer und das Wohnzimmer, die sich im gleichen, zentralen Bereich befinden, sind durch eine feste Struktur voneinander getrennt. In einer Ecke dieses Bereiches befindet sich das Fernseh- und Videogerät und die Stereoanlage, so als ob es sich um eine Verlängerung des Wohnzimmers handelte. Der einheitliche Bodenbelag und die Wände werden durch Oberflächenmaterialien unterbrochen, die vielfältiger und abwechslungsreicher sind.

The dining room stands next to the living room so as not to interrupt either communication or spatial continuity.

La salle à manger est adjacente au salon, pour ne pas interrompre la communication ni la fluidité spatiale.

Das Speisezimmer befindet sich neben dem Wohnzimmer, so dass weder die Kommunikation noch der Fluss des Raumes unterbrochen werden.

The extending table in the kitchen accommodates a variable number of dinner guests.

Dans la cuisine, une table extensible se détache, permettant d'augmenter le nombre de convives si nécessaire.

In der Küche steht ein ausziehbarer Tisch, an dem bei Bedarf mehr Gäste Platz finden.

Post Office in London
Bureau de poste à Londres
Postamt in London

London, UK

The project involved the conversion of a former post office into a painter's apartment and studio. The program required the construction of a living room, kitchen, studio, two bedrooms, two bathrooms, and a roof terrace. Contrary to expectations, the architect, Gunnar Orefelt, decided not to to reserve the double space for the living room and add a mezzanine for the bedrooms, the kitchen, and the bathrooms on two floors, but opted for inverting this arrangement: he reserved the bottom floor for the bedrooms, with bathrooms on one side and a spacious hall with a pool table on the other, and placed the studio in the double-height space. Furthermore, he added a mezzanine overlooking the studio to accommodate the living areas, the kitchen, and the dining room, lit by large skylights.

Le projet concerne la réhabilitation d'un ancien bureau de poste pour établir le studio et la résidence d'une peintre. Le programme requis englobe la construction d'un salon, d'une cuisine, d'un atelier de peinture, de deux chambres à coucher, de deux salles de bains et d'une terrasse de toit. Contrairement à l'habitude, à savoir réserver l'espace double pour le salon et restaurer des combles pour accueillir les chambres à coucher, la cuisine et les salles de bains sur deux étages, Gunnar Orefelt a choisi d'opter pour la conception inverse : le rez-de-chaussée a été réservé pour les chambres à coucher et les salles de bains, d'un côté, avec un ample vestibule comprenant une table de billard, de l'autre. L'espace sur deux hauteurs a été optimisé pour installer le studio. En outre, un espace mansardé accueille les zones du salon, de la cuisine et de la salle à manger, éclairées par de grands velux et donnant sur le studio de peinture.

Ein ehemaliges Postamt wurde zum Atelier und Wohnung einer Malerin umgebaut. Die Kundin wünschte sich ein Wohnzimmer, eine Küche, ein Atelier, zwei Schlafzimmer, zwei Bäder und eine Dachterrasse. Man hätte also erwartet, dass in dem Raum mit doppelter Höhe das Wohnzimmer geschaffen werde, in einer oberen Ebene die Schlafzimmer, Küche und Bäder auf zwei Stockwerken verteilt seien, aber Gunnar Orefelt drehte die Situation um : Im Untergeschoss liegen auf einer Seite die Schlafzimmer und die Bäder, auf der anderen Seite eine weite Empfangshalle mit einem Billardtisch, und man nutzte die hohe Decke, um das Atelier einzurichten. Auf der oberen Ebene, in Form einer Galerie, liegen das Wohnzimmer, die Küche und das Esszimmer. Sie erhalten durch Dachfenster Tageslicht und erlaubenden den Blick auf das Atelier.

The kitchen, the dining room, and the living room are on the mezzanine, lit by skylights and endowed with a view of the studio below.

La cuisine, la salle à manger et le salon se trouvent dans la mansarde supérieure, éclairée par les velux, avec vue sur le studio de peinture du rez-de-chaussée.

Die Küche, das Speisezimmer und das Wohnzimmer befinden sich auf der oberen Ebene. Dort fällt durch Dachfenster Tageslicht ein und man sieht auf das Atelier im Erdgeschoss herab.

The bathroom and bedroom are separated by a glass partition and share the same open space.

La salle de bains et la chambre à coucher sont séparées par une cloison de verre et partagent le même espace ouvert.

Das Bad und das Schlafzimmer, die im gleichen offenen Raum liegen, werden durch einen Wandschirm aus Glas getrennt.

Loft in Bruges
Loft à Bruges
Loft in Brujas

Bruges, Belgium

The most important aspect of the intervention that converted this former tin factory into an apartment was the remodeling of the roof, which consists of a lattice structure supporting a traditional saw-tooth roof. The designers decided to glaze the north slope of each section, thereby increasing the penetration of natural light. Furthermore, given the considerable height of the ceiling, occupants get the impression that they are in an outdoor plaza. On the lower floor, the living room opens on to a small garden with a covered swimming pool. Thanks to the height of the ceiling it was possible to add a mezzanine floor, which contains the kitchen, dining room, bar, and television room. Beneath the mezzanine there is a pool room, a gym, the bedroom, the changing room, and the bathroom, which connects directly with the swimming pool.

Ce qui est essentiel dans la réhabilitation de cette ancienne usine de boîte de conserves, c'est la restructuration de la couverture, formée par une ossature de persiennes qui soutiennent une toiture traditionnelle en forme de dents de montagnes. Les concepteurs ont décidé de remplacer le versant nord de chacune des mini-toitures par une surface de verre. Ceci accroît la luminosité naturelle dans l'habitation. En outre, la hauteur considérable de l'espace, fait que l'habitant a l'impression d'être sur une place extérieure. Au rez-de-chaussée, le salon s'ouvre sur un petit jardin qui accueille une piscine couverte. La hauteur du toit permet de construire une mansarde où se trouvent la cuisine, la salle à manger, le bar et la salle de télévision. Sous les combles, il y a une salle de billard, une salle de gymnastique, la chambre à coucher, le dressing et la salle de bains reliée directement à la piscine.

Der wichtigste Eingriff beim Umbau dieser ehemaligen Konservenfabrik fand am Dach statt, das aus einer Struktur aus Gittern bestand, die ein traditionelles Dach in Form von Sägezähnen trug. Die Gestalter ersetzten die Nordseite jedes Minidaches durch eine verglaste Fläche. So fiel viel mehr Tageslicht in die Wohnung ein, und durch die Höhe der Räume entsteht der Eindruck, dass man sich auf einem Platz im Freien befindet. Im Erdgeschoss öffnet sich das Wohnzimmer zu einem kleinen Garten, in dem sich ein überdachtes Schwimmbad befindet. Die Höhe der Decke ermöglichte die Konstruktion eines Zwischengeschosses, in dem sich die Küche, das Esszimmer, die Bar und das Fernsehzimmer befinden. Unter dem Zwischengeschoss liegen der Billardraum, der Fitnessraum, das Schlafzimmer, das Ankleidezimmer und das Bad, von dem man direkt zum Swimmingpool gelangt.

Thanks to the remodeling of the roof, abundant natural light penetrates to enhance the beauty of the owner's art collection.

La restructuration de la toiture permet à la lumière d'entrer en abondance, exaltant ainsi la beauté des œuvres d'art de la propriétaire.

Durch die Umgestaltung des Daches fällt sehr viel Tageslicht in die Räume, was die Schönheit der Kunstwerke aus dem Besitz des Wohnungseigentümers unterstreicht.

The twenty-foot high ceiling creates a flexible, luminous space.

Les six mètres de hauteur du plafond créent un espace flexible et lumineux.

Durch die sechs Meter Dachhöhe konnte eine flexible und helle Wohnlandschaft geschaffen werden.

The extractor hood in the kitchen hangs from the lattice structure supporting the roof and stretches to the middle of the work table.

La hotte d'extraction de la cuisine pend de la structure à persiennes du toit jusqu'au centre du plan de travail.

Die Dunstabzugshaube in der Küche hängt von der Gitterstruktur des Daches bis zum Zentrum des Arbeitstisches.

Inés Rodríguez, Alfonso de Luna, Norman Cinamond, Carla Cirici

Barcelona, Spain

Vapor Llull

Cristian Cirici & Carles Bassó refurbished a former chemical products plant, consisting of a ground floor and two upper floors, and converted it into apartments. They preserved the exterior brick walls, the vaulted structure, and the timber roof, while adding three blocks of vertical communication consisting of a stairway and goods elevator, to provide independent access to each of the eighteen apartments. The sophistication of the new elements contrasts with the preserved structures and the orange-and-blue painted façade. Cirici & Bassó left the apartments without finishes so that several interior designers might provide their own personal touches to each. The four clearly differentiated projects are the work of designers Inés Rodríguez, Norman Cinamond, Alfonso de Luna and Clara Cirici.

Cristian Cirici & Carles Bassó ont réhabilité une ancienne usine de produits chimiques, avec rez-de-chaussée et deux étages, pour la convertir en habitations. Ils ont conservé les murs extérieurs en brique, les fosses d'entrevous et la couverture de cintres de bois, tout en ajoutant trois blocs de communication verticale formés par un escalier et un monte-charge, afin de créer un accès indépendant à chacune des dix-huit habitations. La sophistication des neufs éléments contraste avec les structures qui ont été préservées et avec la façade peinte en jaune et bleu. Cirici & Bassó ont laissé les habitations sans finitions afin de laisser libre cours aux idées et au regard personnel des décorateurs d'intérieur dans l'agencement de chaque habitation. Les quatre propositions, clairement différenciées entre elles, sont l'œuvre des designers Inés Rodríguez, Norman Cinamond, Alfonso de Luna et Carla Cirici.

Cristian Cirici & Carles Bassó bauten eine ehemalige, dreistöckige Chemiefabrik in Wohnungen um. Die äußeren Ziegelwände, das Mauerwerk der Gewölbe und die Lehrbögen des Daches blieben erhalten. Hinzugefügt wurden drei Blöcke für die vertikale Verbindung, die aus einer Treppe und einem Lastenaufzug bestehen, so dass jede der achtzehn Wohnungen einen unabhängigen Zugang erhielt. Die edlen neuen Elemente stehen zu den alten Strukturen und zu der orange und blau gestrichenen Fassade im Gegensatz. Cirici & Bassó ließen die Wohnungen im Rohbau, damit verschiedene Innenarchitekten ihre Arbeit fortsetzen und in jede Wohnung einen eigenen Stil einbringen konnten. Die vier Vorschläge, die sich deutlich voneinander unterscheiden, stammen von den Innenarchitekten Inés Rodríguez, Norman Cinamond, Alfonso de Luna und Carla Cirici.

One of the essential criteria guiding the development of the project was the preservation of the old building's personality.

Une des principales intentions dans le déroulement du projet est de préserver l'identité de l'ancien établissement.

Eines der wichtigsten Ziele bei dieser Planung war es, die Identität des ehemaligen Gebäudes zu erhalten.

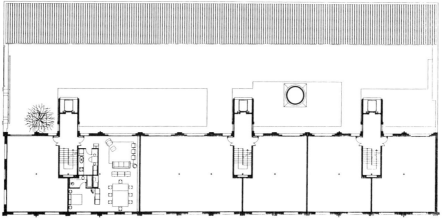

› Plan Plan Grundriss

Norman Cinamond opted for a densely furnished space dominated by various shades of red.

Norman Cinamond a opté pour un espace densément meublé avec une dominance de tons rouges.

Norman Cinamond schuf üppig möblierte Räumlichkeiten bei denen Rottöne vorherrschen.

The use of wood and the tiled flooring create a warm, natural atmosphere.

L'emploi du bois et le carrelage de céramique de tufeau confèrent une ambiance chaleureuse et naturelle.

Holz und der Bodenbelag aus Naturstein schaffen eine warme und natürliche Atmosphäre.

Loft in Old Street
Loft à Old Street
Loft in Old Street

London, UK

One of the fundamental premises of this project was the creation of a single space based on a functional design adaptable to changes. Transparency was the guiding principle of the design, so excessively visible partitions were ruled out to prevent any disruption of the overall effect. The divisions conceived to separate the areas are flexible and multifunctional, and help to maintain the sensation of spaciousness. The public area is split into two areas, three feet apart; the dining room and kitchen occupy the upper part while the living room lies below. The materials were chosen to accentuate the division and enhance the qualities of each space. The meeting point between the public and private areas is marked by a translucent glass wall that sets up various interplays of light.

La conception de ce loft a comme critère de base la création d'un design fonctionnel et modulable au gré des modifications de l'habitation. La notion de diaphanéité est omniprésente, évitant les cloisons trop visibles qui gênent la perception globale de l'ensemble. Les partitions conçues pour les pièces sont flexibles et à fonctions multiples, contribuant à maintenir la sensation d'ampleur. La zone publique présente une dénivellation de plus d'un mètre : la salle à manger et la cuisine occupent la partie supérieure et le salon, l'inférieure. Les matériaux ont été choisis afin de servir à accentuer la division et de souligner les avantages de chaque espace. L'axe qui réunit la zone publique à la zone privée prend la forme d'un mur en verre translucide qui crée différents jeux de lumière.

Bei der Gestaltung dieses Lofts wünschten sich die Kunden vor allem einen einzigen Raum mit funktionalem Design, den man nach den Bedürfnissen der Bewohner verändern kann. Er sollte transparent und durchgehend wirken, deshalb wurden sehr diskrete Raumteilungen eingesetzt, die das Gesamtbild des Raumes nicht stören. Die Raumteiler, die man dazu entwarf, dienen zum Abtrennen von flexiblen und multifunktionellen Bereichen, ohne das Gefühl von Weite zu beeinträchtigen. Der von allen benutzte Bereich weist einen Höhenunterschied von über einem Meter auf: Speisezimmer und Küche liegen auf der oberen Ebene und das Wohnzimmer auf der unteren. Die Materialien wurden so gewählt, dass sie die Raumaufteilung unterstreichen und die Eigenschaften jedes Bereiches hervorheben. Der von allen benutzte Bereich und die Privaträume treffen an einer Wand aus lichtdurchlässigen Glas zusammen, was interessante Lichteffekte erzeugt.

The kitchen and dining room share the same open space, bounded by the drop down to the living room.

La cuisine et la salle à manger partagent le même espace ouvert, délimité par la dénivellation du salon.

Die Küche und das Speisezimmer liegen im gleichen offenen Raum, der von dem Höhenunterschied begrenzt wird, den es zum Wohnzimmer gibt.

Loft in Berlin
Loft à Berlin
Loft in Berlin

Berlin, Germany

The designers of this apartment sought to create a voluminous space in which the homogenous finishes and astute choice of materials would guarantee a warm, comfortable environment. To differentiate the various functions, decorative elements have been strategically placed to indicate the use of each area. The spaces for domestic use are located next to the main façade in order to take maximum advantage of the sunlight. The dining room, at one end, is characterized by the arrangement of elements on a rug that marks out the space. Next to it stands the kitchen, which occupies the center and serves as a link with the dining room. A stairway leads majestically up from the living room to the apartment's private quarters. The master bedroom evokes the essence of the project: light, warmth and transparency.

Ce projet d'habitation cherche à créer un vaste espace où l'harmonie des finitions et le bon choix des matériaux garantissent une ambiance chaleureuse et confortable. Afin de différencier les fonctions, des éléments de décorations ont été placés à des points stratégiques démarquant ainsi chaque pièce. Les espaces à usage domestique ont été placés à côté de la façade principale pour optimiser le flux de lumière. La salle à manger, à l'une des extrémités, se définit par la disposition des éléments sur un tapis qui délimite ainsi l'espace. Juste à côté, la cuisine occupe un espace central et sert de lien avec la salle à manger. Un escalier s'élève majestueusement depuis le salon, conduisant vers les espaces privés. La chambre à coucher principale représente l'essence du projet, à savoir, lumière, chaleur et transparence.

Dieses Loft in Berlin wurde in eine großzügige Wohnumgebung umgestaltet, in der durch die Einheitlichkeit der Oberfläche und die sorgfältige Auswahl der Materialien eine warme und einladende Atmosphäre herrscht. Um die verschiedenen Funktionen der einzelnen Zonen voneinander abzugrenzen, wurden strategisch dekorative Elemente verteilt, die die Funktion jedes Bereichs markieren. Die Bereiche für häusliche Funktionen liegen hintereinander an der Hauptfassade, um das einfallende Licht maximal auszunutzen. Im Esszimmer an einem Ende wurden die Elemente auf einem Teppich angeordnet, der die Begrenzungen markiert. Daneben liegt die Küche, die den zentralen Raum einnimmt und die Verbindung zum Esszimmer herstellt. Eine Treppe steigt majestätisch aus dem Wohnzimmer auf und führt in die privateren Räume der Wohnung. Das große Schlafzimmer spiegelt die Essenz der Wohnung wider, Licht, Wärme und Transparenz.

The living room is bathed in natural light that penetrates through large windows, although an opaque panel makes it possible to filter light when necessary.

Le salon bénéficie de la lumière naturelle dispensée par les grandes baies vitrées, bien qu'un panneau opaque permette de tamiser l'entrée de la lumière si nécessaire.

Durch große Fenster fällt viel Licht ins Wohnzimmer. Durch ein lichtundurchlässiges Paneel kann das Licht jedoch gedämpft werden.

This space behind the living room acts as an extension of the rest area.

Cet espace, situé derrière le salon, se transforme en extension de la zone de repos.

Hinter dem Wohnzimmer wird dieser Raum zu einer Verlängerung der Ruhezone.

The judicious selection of materials and the impeccable finishes create a warm, comfortable environment.

Le choix judicieux des matériaux et les finitions impeccables créent un espace chaud et confortable.

Durch eine sorgfältige Auswahl der Materialien und reine Oberflächen wirkt der Raum warm und einladend.

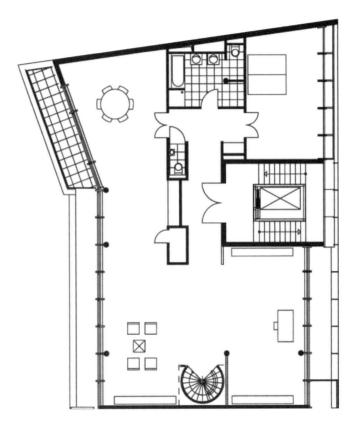

The kitchen, which stands in the middle of the apartment, lures visitors into the living room at the other end.

La cuisine, située au centre de l'espace, invite à entrer au salon, installé à l'extrémité inverse.

Die Küche in der Mitte des Raumes lädt dazu ein, in das Wohnzimmer am anderen Ende weiterzugehen.

The sloping windows focus attention on the bedroom, which is bathed in natural light.

L'inclinaison des fenêtres invite à découvrir la chambre à coucher qui bénéficie d'une bonne luminosité naturelle.

Durch die Neigung der Fenster entdeckt man das Schlafzimmer, in das reichlich Licht einfällt.

The bathroom walls are clad with gray ceramic tiles.

Les parements de la salle de bains sont revêtus de céramiques grises.

Die Wände im Badezimmer sind mit grauen Keramikplatten verkleidet.

Apartment in Melbourne
Habitation à Melbourne
Wohnung in Melbourne

Melbourne, Australia

The initial idea governing this remodeling operation was to preserve the building's original character. The existing concrete columns, the beams, the ceiling, and the walls of the living room and entrance were deliberately left where they were. A false plaster ceiling was added only to the kitchen and bathrooms. A number of complementary light sources were installed to provide diffused illumination. As the transparency of the space has been maintained, its original scale has not been lost. The walls of the main room and the bathrooms were demolished to obtain a continuous ceiling that visually connects all the rooms. The privacy of these rooms was ensured by the placement of glazed panels that separate their functions. The materials were strategically selected to enhance the industrial character of the apartment.

Dès le départ, la restructuration de cet espace a prévu de conserver le caractère original de l'édifice : les colonnes de béton existantes, les poutres, le toit et les murs de la zone du salon et de l'entrée ont été sciemment conservés. Seul, un faux plafond de plâtre a été installé dans la cuisine et dans les salles de bains. Certains points d'éclairage additionnel permettent de diffuser la lumière dans l'ensemble des pièces. L'espace, conservant son caractère diaphane, ne perd pas son échelle initiale. Les murs de l'habitation principale et des salles de bains ont été démolis pour obtenir une toiture unique et continue qui connecte visuellement tous les espaces entre eux. L'intimité nécessaire à ces pièces est préservée grâce à des panneaux de verre séparant les fonctions. Les matériaux ont été soigneusement choisis pour accentuer le caractère industriel de l'habitation.

Bei der Umgestaltung dieser Wohnung sollte der ursprüngliche Charakter des Gebäudes erhalten bleiben. Die existierenden Betonsäulen, die Balken, die Decke und die Wände im Wohnzimmer und am Eingang wurden so erhalten, wie sie einst waren. Es wurde nur eine zweite Decke aus Gips in der Küche und in den Bädern eingezogen. Einige zusätzliche Lichtquellen wurden installiert, die gedämpftes Licht verbreiten. Da der Raum sehr offen und transparent ist, gingen auch die ursprünglichen Abmessungen nicht verloren. Die Wände des großen Schlafzimmers und der Bäder wurden abgerissen, um eine einzige, durchgehende Decke zu schaffen, die visuell alle Räume miteinander verbindet. Die notwendige Privatsphäre in diesen Räumen wird durch verglaste Paneele erreicht, die verschiedene Arten von Bereichen trennen. Die Materialien wurden so ausgewählt, dass der industrielle Charakter der Wohnung erhalten blieb.

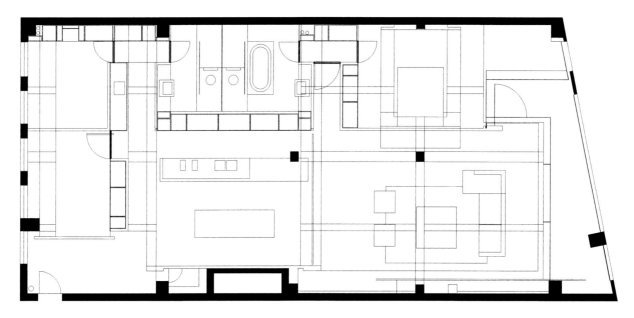

› Plan Plan Grundriss

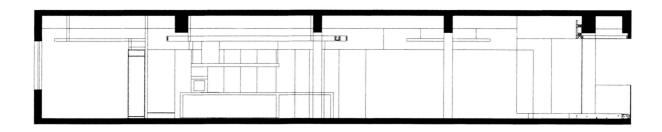

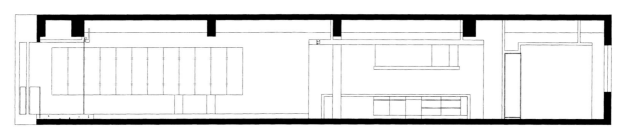

› Sections Sections Schnitte

Various separation mechanisms, such as open partitions or glazed panels, permit unencumbered movement through the domestic space.

Les différents mécanismes de séparation, à l'instar de cloisons ouvertes ou de panneaux de verre, permettent de maintenir la fluidité des espaces domestiques.

Die verschiedenen Trennmechanismen wie offene Zwischenwände oder verglaste Paneele sorgen für eine fließende Verbindung zwischen allen Wohnbereichen.

House in Frenchs Forest
Maison à Frenchs Forest
Haus in Frenchs Forest

Sydney, Australia

The restauration and enlargement of this house reponded to the needs of a growing family while presenting an innovative look. Its location, on one of the beaches north of the city, served as a source of inspiration for the architects, since the new design featured a three-level roof whose complex, expressive outline alludes to surfing. The curved forms that the roof creates inside mark the entrance, separate the different settings and configure the central stairway, which is the focal point of the project. The outcome is a flowing, flexible space characterized by the contrast of bright colors perfectly integrated into the white background of the walls and ceiling. Constructional elements such as the high ceilings allow the light to flood the different environments.

La restauration et l'agrandissement de cette maison devaient satisfaire les besoins d'une famille en croissance, tout en offrant une image novatrice. Les architectes se sont inspirés de l'implantation sur les plages du nord de la ville, car la nouvelle conception prévoit une toiture sur trois niveaux créant une silhouette complexe et expressive faisant allusion à la culture du surf. Les formes courbes créées par la toiture à l'intérieur, délimitent l'accès, différencient les divers univers et forment l'escalier central, point de mire du projet. Il en résulte un espace fluide et polyvalent qui fait ressortir les contrastes de couleurs vives parfaitement intégrées sur le fond blanc des murs et du toit. La lumière tire parti des paramètres constructifs, comme les toits tout en hauteur, qui permettent à la lumière d'inonder à sa guise les divers espaces de vie.

Die Renovierung und Erweiterung dieses Hauses war notwendig, da die Familie wuchs. Gleichzeitig sollte das Gesamtbild erneuert werden. Das Haus befindet sich an einem Strand im Norden der Stadt, was die Architekten dazu inspirierte, ein Dach auf drei Ebenen zu schaffen, dessen ausdrucksvolle Silhouette auf das Windsurfen anspielt. Die Kurvenlinien des Daches markieren im Inneren den Zugang, unterscheiden die verschiedenen Bereiche voneinander und bilden die zentral gelegene Treppe, die der Mittelpunkt der Planung ist. Es entstand ein fließender und kosmopolitischer Raum, in dem starke Farben miteinander im Kontrast stehen, die sich perfekt in den weißen Hintergrund, den die Wände und das Dach bilden, integrieren. Das Licht unterstreicht noch die tragenden Wände und die hohen Decken. Alle Bereiche der Wohnung werden von Tageslicht durchflutet.

The lounge, dining room and kitchen share the same space, with no partitions to hinder communication.

Le salon, la salle à manger et la cuisine partagent un espace commun, sans cloisonnement qui puisse enfreindre la communication.

Das Wohnzimmer, das Speisezimmer und die Küche befinden sich im gleichen Raum ohne Trennwände, um die Verbindung nicht zu unterbrechen.

The materials and finishes are proof of the refinement applied to each area.

Les matériaux et finitions sont une preuve de l'expression épurée présente dans chaque pièce.

Die Materialien und Oberflächen sind so gewählt, dass jede einzelne Umgebung sehr klar und rein wirkt.

The stairway, which links the different floors, endows the central space with dynamism and expressiveness.

La planification dynamique et expressive de l'espace central provient de l'escalier reliant les étages de l'habitation.

Der dynamische und ausdrucksvolle Grundriss des zentralen Raumes entsteht durch die Treppe, die die verschiedenen Etagen des Hauses miteinander verbindet.

The rooms are functional spaces far removed from conventionalism.

Les pièces recréent des espaces fonctionnels en dehors des standards habituels.

Die Zimmer sind funktionelle und sehr ungewöhnliche und interessant gestaltete Räume.

Lloyd Loft
Loft Lloyd
Loft Lloyd

San Francisco, USA

The architects responsible for remodeling this loft pursued three main objectives. The first was to eliminate all dark, oppressive spaces by demolishing several partitions and installing skylights and a glazed cavity two stories high. The second consisted of designing a gallery to serve as the backdrop to the client's substantial art collection. And the third was to build a set of built-in closets for maintenance equipment, the sound system and other installations, so that when not in use their presence would be sculptural and unobtrusive. A masonry stairway with wooden steps was fitted between the wall and a glazed screen that rises up to the floor above, which accommodates the dining and living rooms and provides access to the terrace. This screen serves as a wall but allows light to flow through freely.

Les architectes responsables de la restructuration de ce loft se sont fixés trois objectifs majeurs. Le premier étant d'éliminer tous les espaces sombres et oppressants existants après avoir enlevé maintes cloisons et installé des velux et une cavité tout en verre de deux étages de hauteur. Le deuxième consiste à concevoir une galerie qui serve de toile de fond pour exposer l'importante collection d'art de la cliente. Le troisième objectif, enfin, étant de construire une série d'armoires encastrées, contenant les nombreuses installations, les appareils d'entretien et sonores de tout le loft. Lorsqu'elles ne sont pas utilisées, elles occupent l'espace sobrement, de manière sculpturale. Un escalier, doté de marches en bois, est encastré entre le mur et l'écran de verre qui se hausse vers le niveau supérieur où se trouvent la salle à manger et le salon doté d'un accès vers une terrasse. Cet écran, à l'instar d'un mur transparent, permet à la lumière d'entrer librement.

Die Architekten, die dieses Loft umbauten, hatten sich drei Hauptziele gesetzt. Zunächst sollten alle existierenden, dunklen und bedrückenden Räume beseitigt werden, indem Trennwände entfernt und Dachfenster und ein verglaster Hohlraum geschaffen wurden. Das zweite Ziel war die Gestaltung einer Galerie, die als Ausstellungsort für die umfassende Kunstsammlung der Kunden diente. Schließlich konstruierte man noch eine Reihe von Einbauschränken, in denen die zahlreichen Apparate für die Unterhaltung und zum Musik hören untergebracht sind. Diese haben, wenn sie nicht benutzt werden, eine skulpturelles und schlichtes Erscheinungsbild. Eine gemauerte Treppe mit Holzstufen befindet sich zwischen der Wand und einem verglastem Schirm, der bis in das obere Geschoss reicht, wo sich das Esszimmer, das Wohnzimmer und eine Tür zur Terrasse befinden. Dieser Schirm dient als Mauer, die gleichzeitig das Licht hindurch lässt.

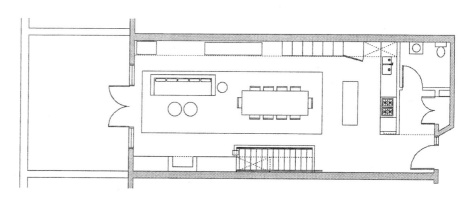

› Ground floor   Rez-de-chaussée   Erdgeschoss

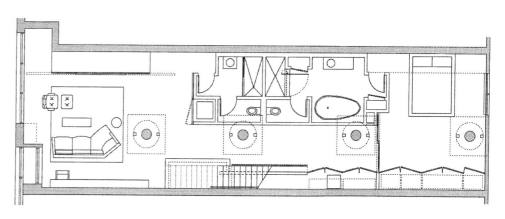

› First floor   Premier étage   Erstes Obergeschoss

The absence of vertical dividers and the use of built-in closets ensure that the large space is well arranged.

L'absence de parements verticaux et la capacité de rangement des armoires encastrées garantissent un espace vaste et bien agencé.

Da keine vertikalen Trennwände vorhanden sind und viele Objekte in Einbauschränken untergebracht sind, wirkt der Raum weit und geordnet.

The living room leads on to the terrace, which serves as an outdoor dining room. Artworks belonging to the client are on display in the bedroom and bathroom.

Le salon s'ouvre sur la terrasse, permettant de prendre les repas en plein air. Dans la chambre à coucher et dans la salle de bains, des œuvres d'art appartenant au propriétaire y sont exposées.

Das Wohnzimmer hat einen Ausgang zur Terrasse, die auch als Esszimmer im Freien dient. Im Schlafzimmer und im Bad werden Kunstwerke aus der Sammlung der Familie ausgestellt.

Goldberg Apartment
Appartement Goldberg
Appartement Goldberg

Sydney, Australia

This apartment, set in a building from the 1920s facing the sea, was designed for a couple who needed space in which to accommodate guests at their regular social gatherings. With this end in view, most of the interior divisions were eliminated to generate an open space adapted to the new requirements, whose social area is closely linked to the kitchen. This public space is separated from the private areas - two bedrooms, a bathroom and a study - by a kind of timber-clad wall that doubles as a closet due to its considerable width. The set of false ceilings contains a complex lighting system and defines the different environments in the spacious social area. The homogeneous materials and uniform flooring make for a placid, serene interior.

Cet appartement situé dans un édifice des années vingt, orienté vers la mer, a été conçu pour un couple qui avait besoin d'espaces plus généreux pour accueillir leurs hôtes, protagonistes de leur vie sociale. A cette fin, la plupart des cloisons intérieures ont été éliminées pour créer un espace ouvert adapté aux nouveaux besoins, tout en gardant une étroite relation avec la cuisine. Cet espace public est séparé de la sphère privée -deux chambres, une salle de bains et un studio- par une sorte de mur revêtu de bois qui, en outre, fonctionne comme une armoire dotée d'une capacité intérieure considérable. Les multiples faux plafonds accueillent un système complet d'éclairage et définissent les divers univers à l'intérieur de la grande zone commune. L'uniformité des matériaux et la continuité du carrelage déclinent un intérieur emprunt de calme et de sérénité.

Dieses Appartement in einem zum Meer liegenden Gebäude aus den Zwanzigerjahren wurde für ein Paar entworfen, das viel Platz braucht, um seine Gäste unterzubringen, da es gerne und oft Besuch hat. Deshalb wurden die meisten inneren Raumteiler entfernt und ein offener Raum entworfen, der zu diesem Zweck geeignet ist. Die Küche ist mit diesem Bereich, der für die Zusammenkünfte dient, eng verbunden. Dieser von allen genutzte Raum ist von den privateren Räumen, zwei Schlafzimmern, einem Bad und einem Atelier, durch eine Art mit Holz verkleidete Wand getrennt, die gleichzeitig als Schrank dient, der viel Platz im Inneren hat. In den verschiedenen eingezogenen Decken ist ein komplettes Beleuchtungssystem untergebracht. Sie definieren die verschiedenen Bereiche innerhalb des großen Raumes. Durch die Einheitlichkeit der Materialien und den durchgehenden Bodenbelag entstand eine ruhige und gelassene Atmosphäre.

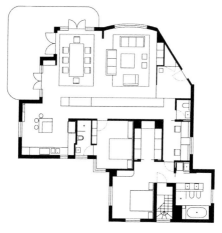

› Plan Plan Grundriss

Functions seem to merge as a result of the homogeneous flooring and the contrast between the different kinds of wood.

Les fonctions semblent se confondre grâce à l'uniformité du carrelage et au contraste entre les différents types de bois.

Die verschiedenen Funktionen scheinen durch den durchgehenden Fußbodenbelag, der einen Kontrast zu den verschiedenen verwendeten Holzsorten bildet, zu verschmelzen.

The large wooden element rationalizes the different environments while also serving as a closet.

Le grand élément en bois rationalise la distribution des divers espaces de vie tout en jouant le rôle de zone de rangement.

Das große Holzelement rationalisiert die verschiedenen Bereiche und dient gleichzeitig als Lagerraum.

Penthouse in East Village
Attique à East Village
Dachwohnung East Village

New York, USA

The refurbishment of this apartment took advantage of the split-level original structure to organize the various parts of the domestic program. The renovation of the top floor involved building a small terrace in the attic with the main entrance and is directly linked to the living and dining rooms. The creation of an open, uncluttered outdoor space allows natural light to bathe the interior, while establishing a correlation with the exterior elements. This space, a continuation of the main dining room, constitutes a meeting place around which the remaining private rooms are arranged. From the middle of the main floor it is possible to perceive how the different levels, projected from the floor above, descend in a geometrical and volumetric interplay that captures the essence of the space. This volumetric interplay is made possible by the height of the ceiling.

La restauration de cette habitation a profité des dénivellations offertes par la structure initiale pour organiser les différentes parties du programme intérieur. La rénovation de l'étage supérieur a permis de créer une petite terrasse dans l'attique qui héberge l'entrée principale, directement connectée au salon et à la salle à manger. La création d'une zone extérieure ouverte et spacieuse permet à la lumière directe d'inonder l'intérieur de l'habitation, tout en instaurant une relation entre les éléments extérieurs. En prolongement de la salle à manger principale, cet espace se transforme en un centre de réunions autour duquel s'articule le reste des espaces privés. Depuis le centre de l'étage principal, on aperçoit deux niveaux distincts qui se projettent depuis l'étage supérieur et qui descendent en un jeu de géométries et de volumes capturant l'essence de l'espace. Ce jeu volumétrique est possible grâce à l'importante hauteur du plafond.

Bei der Renovierung dieser Wohnung nutzte man die Höhenunterschiede der Originalstruktur, um die verschiedenen Wohnfunktionen räumlich zu verteilen. Bei der Renovierung des oberen Stockwerks, auf dem der Haupteingang liegt, der direkt mit dem Wohnzimmer und Esszimmer verbunden ist, schuf man eine kleine Dachterrasse. Durch die Schaffung einer offenen Zone im Freien fällt viel Tageslicht direkt in die Wohnung und es entsteht eine Beziehung zu den Elementen im Freien. Wie eine Fortsetzung des eigentlichen Esszimmers wird dieser Bereich zum Treffpunkt, um den herum alle anderen Räume liegen. Im Zentrum des unteren Stockwerks nimmt man wahr, wie die verschiedenen Ebenen, die vom oberen Stockwerk aus geplant wurden, in einem geometrischen Spiel mit den Formen herabsteigen und die Essenz des Raumes auffangen. Dieses Spiel mit den Formen ist möglich, da die Decke sehr hoch ist.

The large bay window allows natural light to flood into the interior.

L'immense baie vitrée située dans le salon permet à la lumière d'envahir l'intérieur.

Das große Fenster im Wohnzimmer lässt sehr viel Tageslicht ins Innere strömen.

Natoma Street Loft
Loft Natoma Street
Loft Natoma Street

San Francisco, USA

The initial purpose of the project was to create a two-story volume that would make it possible to locate the main room on a higher level, conceived as a mezzanine. A broad view of the apartment - which opens to the exterior through a window overlooking the terrace - is available from any point on the perimeter. The architects were required to conceive a modern home adaptable to the lifestyle of its owners. To achieve this goal, thei chose their main material, creating an effect of modernity throughout the loft. Another predominant construction element is the half-height partition, consisting of a lower part in masonry and an upper part in glass, which allows natural light to flow through the apartment. This device was feasible as a result of the considerable height of the ceilings; furthermore, these partitions enhance the feeling of spaciousness.

Ce projet d'habitation a prévu dès le départ de créer un volume de deux étages pour permettre de situer l'habitation principale sur le niveau le plus élevé, conçu comme une mansarde. Il était nécessaire de maintenir partout la vue vaste et dégagée sur l'habitation, ouverte vers l'extérieur grâce à une baie vitrée donnant sur la terrasse. Les architectes ont été chargés de concevoir une habitation moderne et modulable au gré des habitudes de ses propriétaires. Pour y parvenir, ils ont eu principalement recours à l'acier, créant un effet de modernisme dans tout le loft. Des cloisons à mi-hauteur sont un autre exemple d'élément constructif prédominant, la partie inférieure étant en maçonnerie et le reste en verre. Cette solution favorise le flux de lumière naturelle dans toutes les pièces. La hauteur considérable des plafonds a permis de réaliser cette idée qui contribue à intensifier la sensation d'espace.

Bei diesem Umbau sollte eine zweistöckige Wohnung entstehen, in der das Hauptschlafzimmer sich auf der höchsten Ebene, einer Art Mansarde, befindet. Von jedem Punkt aus sollte die Wohnung weit und groß wirken, was durch ein großes Fenster zur Terrasse erreicht wurde. Die Architekten entwarfen eine moderne Wohnung, die man einfach an die Gewohnheiten der Wohnungseigentümer anpassen kann. Dazu benutzten sie vor allem Stahl, der das Gesamtbild des Lofts sehr modern wirken lässt. Andere vorherrschende Konstruktionselemente sind Trennwände auf halber Höhe, die unten aus Mauerwerk und oben aus Glas sind, so dass Licht in alle Räume fällt. Dies war möglich, da die Decke sehr hoch ist. So wirkt das gesamte Loft sehr groß.

In order to allow natural light to penetrate, the architects turned to functional solutions such as the translucent panels placed at different points in the apartment.

Pour favoriser l'entrée de la lumière, les concepteurs ont eu recours à des solutions fonctionnelles, comme les panneaux translucides installés en différents points de l'habitation.

Damit das Licht in alle Räume fällt, wurden Elemente wie lichtdurchlässige Paneele an verschiedenen Punkten der Wohnung eingesetzt.

Steel was chosen as one of the predominant materials in order to obtain an effect that is both modern and austere.

L'acier est un des moyens principaux employés dans ce projet pour obtenir un effet à la fois moderne et austère.

Stahl ist eines der wichtigsten Elemente in diesem Loft. Er lässt die Wohnumgebung modern und gleichzeitig schlicht wirken.

317

Lofts in Gràcia
Lofts à Gràcia
Lofts in Gràcia

Barcelona, Spain

The two apartments that constitute this project represent two different conceptions of the loft-home. In one of them, most of the structural elements have been left bare (the ceiling vaults, the façade wall, and the beams). The apartment consists of two areas arranged on a single floor: a strip that contains the bedrooms and bathrooms, and a large square sitting room, one of the corners of which is closed off to isolate the kitchen. In the other loft it was decided to paint the walls yellow. In this case, the apartment consists of a double-height living room that includes an open-plan kitchen and a slide zone split into three levels. The lower floor contains the dining room, the staircase, and a toilet; the mezzanine is occupied by the master bedroom, the dressing room, and the bathroom. The independent top floor is given over to the children and holds two bedrooms, a bathroom, and a play room.

Les deux appartements de ce projet représentent deux visions différentes de l'habitation-loft. Dans l'un d'eux, la majorité des éléments structuraux ont été laissés tels quels (les entrevous du toit, le mur de la façade, les poutres de treillis). L'appartement comprend deux aires distribuées sur un seul niveau : une frange qui accueille les chambres à coucher et les salles de bain et une grande salle carrée dont l'un des angles se ferme pour rendre la cuisine indépendante du reste. Dans l'autre loft, les murs ont été délibérément peints en jaune. Ici, l'habitation est formée d'un salon à double hauteur, comprenant une cuisine ouverte et une zone latérale divisée en trois niveaux. Le rez-de-chaussée héberge la salle à manger, l'escalier et un cabinet de toilettes. La mezzanine accueille la chambre à coucher principale, le dressing et la salle de bains. Enfin, il existe un troisième niveau indépendant, destiné aux enfants, avec deux chambres à coucher, une salle de bains et une salle de jeux.

Die beiden Wohnungen, die hier vorgestellt werden, zeigen zwei verschiedene Herangehensweisen an den Wohungstyp Loft. In einer der Wohnung sind fast alle Strukturelemente ohne Verkleidung. Die Wohnung besteht aus zwei Bereichen, die auf einer einzigen Etage liegen. In einer Zone liegen die Schlafzimmer und Bäder, und in der anderen ein großes, quadratisches Wohnzimmer, in dem eine Ecke geschlossen ist, um die Küche abzutrennen. In dem anderen Loft sind die Wände Gelb gestrichen. Diese Wohnung besteht aus einem Wohnzimmer doppelter Höhe, in dem sich eine offene Küche befindet, und aus einer seitlichen Zone, die in drei Ebenen unterteilt ist. Im Untergeschoss befinden sich das Esszimmer und ein Badezimmer, im Obergeschoss liegen das Schlafzimmer, das Ankleidezimmer und das Bad. Schließlich gibt es noch eine dritte, unabhängige Ebene für die Kinder, auf der die Schlafzimmer, ein Bad und ein Spielzimmer liegen.

› Plan   Plan   Grundriss

The design of the partitions, which do not reach the ceiling, creates a sensation of uninterrupted space.

La conception de cloisons qui ne parviennent pas jusqu'au plafond permet de transmettre une sensation d'espace continu.

Es wurden halbhohe Zwischenwände geschaffen, um den Raum ununterbrochen wirken zu lassen.

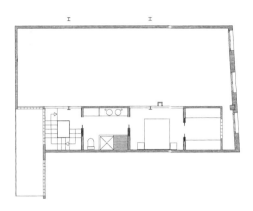

› Ground floor   Rez-de-chaussée   Erdgeschoss

› First floor   Premier étage   Erstes Obergeschoss

› Second floor   Deuxième étage   Zweites Obergeschoss

The bare brick column hides the drainpipes.

La colonne en briques apparentes abrite le passage des tuyaux d'eaux usées.

In der Säule aus unverputztem Ziegelstein befinden sich die Abwasserleitungen.

321

In all the rooms, an interplay is established between yellow-painted surfaces and specific elements finished in golden brown.

On retrouve dans toutes les pièces un jeu chromatique entre les surfaces peintes en jaune, certains éléments et les finitions dans des tons ocre foncé.

In allen Räumen entstand ein Farbenspiel zwischen den gelb gestrichenen Flächen und bestimmten Elementen mit einem dunkleren Ton.

Apartment in São Paulo
Appartement à São Paulo
Appartement in São Paulo

São Paulo, Brazil

This apartment, designed for a famous advertising executive, occupies the two top stories of a building and is divided into three distinct areas. In the first place, the children's quarters, which include the bedrooms and the television and computer room. This same level contains the living area and the communal spaces: sitting room, dining room, kitchen, and washroom. The floor above holds the client's private spaces, which open on to a terrace with a swimming pool. It was not the domestic program, but rather the place ment of the artworks and collector's pieces, that made conceptual demands on the designers. The main objective was to ensure that they were arranged flexibly without cluttering the space, altering it while also embellishing it. To this end, the paintings hang from rails by steel cables that may be freely displaced.

Cet appartement occupant les deux derniers étages d'un édifice, a été dessiné par un fameux publiciste. L'habitation s'articule sur trois zones distinctes. En premier lieu, celle des enfants avec les chambres à coucher et une pièce de télévision et d'ordinateur. Sur ce même niveau, il y a aussi les piéces communes : salon, salle à manger, cuisine et chambre froide. L'étage supérieur accueille les espaces privés du client qui communiquent avec une terrasse dotée d'une piscine. Le projet ne présente pas de conception particulière ment recherchée en ce qui concerne le programme domestique. L'accent a été surtout mis sur l'emplacement de diverses œuvres d'art et objets de la collectionneuse. L'objectif principal étant que l'emplacement de ces éléments soit modulable, sans entraver l'espace, qu'ils ne modifient pas mais qu'ils embellissent. De cette manière, les tableaux sont suspendus à des rails sur câble d'aciers qui se déplacent librement.

Diese Wohnung erstreckt sich über die beiden letzten Stockwerke eines Gebäudes und wurde für einen berühmten Publizisten entworfen. Die Wohnung ist in drei verschiedene Bereiche unterteilt. Zunächst haben die Kinder ihren eigenen Bereich mit Schlafzimmern und einem Spielzimmer. Auf der gleichen Ebene liegen das Wohnzimmer und die Räume mit gemeinsamen Funktionen, also das Wohnzimmer, das Speisezimmer, die Küche. Im oberen Geschoss liegen die privateren Räume des Kunden. Von hier aus gelangt man auf eine Terrasse mit Swimmingpool. Bei der Planung wurden die Anstrengungen vor allem auf die Unterbringun der verschiedenen Kunstwerke und Objekte des Wohnungseigentümers gelegt. Hauptziel war es, für all diese Elemente einen flexiblen Standort zu finden, der im Raum kein Hindernis darstellt, sondern ihn verändert und verschönert. Man hängte deshalb die Bilder mit Stahlseilen an Schicnen auf.

The collector's pieces are contained in display cases so that they do not disrupt the overall effect but are still given the prominence they deserve.

Les divers objets de collection ont été placés dans des vitrines pour ne pas entraver la perception d'ensemble et pour être mis en valeur à leur juste mesure.

Die verschiedenen Objekte aus der Sammlung der Eigentümer befinden sich in Vitrinen, die das Gesamtbild nicht stören und die Bedeutung haben, die ihnen zusteht.

The meticulously calculated lighting and use of supplementary spotlights embellish the works displayed in the different rooms.

Un éclairage très bien étudié et l'emploi de foyers lumineux additionnels embellissent les œuvres exposées à divers endroits.

Die Beleuchtung wurde sehr intelligent verteilt, so dass die Kunstwerke in den verschiedenen Räumen durch zusätzliche Strahler verschönert werden.

Carlson

New York, USA

This loft, housed in a former industrial building, preserves the original structure in the row of iron columns that crosses from one side to the other, and in the high ceilings, which were restored. Acomplished lighting and the open arrangement of elements prevail in the design of this spacious dwelling. The dining room, sitting room, and kitchen are on the south façade, while the bedroom and study, which occasionally doubles as a guest bedroom, stand at the opposite end. In order to preserve the spaciousness of the loft, pivoting floor-to-ceiling doors were designed to ensure uninterrupted views of the whole space. The bedrooms and bathrooms, which require greater privacy, are located at one end of the apartment and partially separated by translucent glazing and wood. In order to enhance the spatial continuity, the flooring material is the same throughout.

Ce loft, situé dans un ancien édifice industriel, conserve le caractère initial de sa structure avec l'enfilade de colonnes de fer qui traverse la surface et ses plafonds tout en hauteur, qui ont été restaurés. Malgré l'ampleur de l'espace, la conception insiste sur le bon éclairage et la disposition ouverte des éléments. La salle à manger, le salon et la cuisine se trouvent sur la façade sud, tandis que la chambre et le studio, utilisé parfois comme chambre d'amis, se trouvent sur le côté opposé. Des portes pivotantes qui vont du sol vers le plafonds permettent de maintenir l'amplitude spatiale du loft et d'avoir une vue dégagée de l'ensemble. Les chambres et les salles de bains, nécessitant davantage d'intimité, sont situées à une des extrémités de l'habitation et partiellement séparées par de grandes surfaces alliant verre et bois. Pour exalter la continuité spatiale, toute la superficie est revêtue du même matériau.

Dieses Loft in einem alten Industriegebäude hat seinen ursprünglichen Charakter erhalten. Die Struktur besteht aus einer Reihe von Eisensäulen, die die Fläche durchkreuzt, und die hohen Decken wurden renoviert. In dem sehr großen Raum legte man viel Wert auf eine gute Beleuchtung und eine offene Anordnung der Elemente. Das Speisezimmer, das Wohnzimmer und die Küche liegen im südlichen Teil der Wohnung, das Schlafzimmer und das Atelier, das manchmal als Gästezimmer dient, befinden sich auf der anderen Seite. Um das Loft weit wirken zu lassen, wurden Schwingtüren entworfen, die vom Boden bis zur Decke reichen und das Gesamtbild frei wirken lassen. Die Zimmer und die Bäder, die mehr Privatsphäre verlangen, befinden sich am Ende der Wohnung und sind teilweise durch lichtdurchlässige Glasflächen und Holz abgetrennt. Um die räumliche Kontinuität zu unterstreichen, ist der gesamte Bodenbelag aus dem gleichen Material.

For the sake of openness, glazed walls were placed to guarantee visual continuity from any point in the apartment.

Des parois en verre conservent l'ouverture de l'espace et favorisent la continuité visuelle à n'importe quel endroit de l'habitation.

Um die Offenheit des Raumes zu bewahren, wurden verglaste Trennwände geschaffen, die eine visuelle Kontinuität von jedem Punkt der Wohnung aus gewähren.

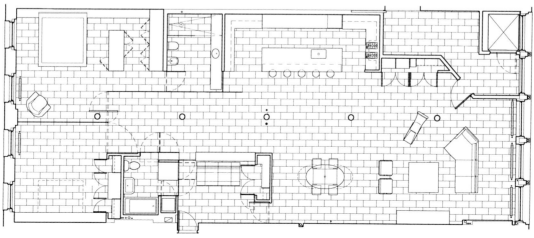

› Plan Plan Grundriss

House in Belmont
Maison à Belmont
Haus in Belmont

San Francisco, USA

In contrast with pseudo-historical reproductions, this house on a hill explores the fusion between two forms of vernacular architecture typical of the region: the mobile trailer-home and Mexican architecture. A long belvedere with its blue stucco wall leads visitors toward a colossal rusted steel door. This door opens into the hall, where a staircase leads up to the floor above. Emulating Mexican vernacular architecture, the ground floor is characterized by walls that convey heaviness in terms of both texture and color. This floor accommodates the master bedroom at one end, an office at the other, and a central area occupied by the dining room, kitchen, and library. The floor above, more inspired by the industrial generation of mobile homes, is a rectangular volume dominated by metal.

Cette habitation située sur une colline explore, à la différence de reproductions historiques superficielles, la fusion de deux architectures populaires typiques de la région : la maison/caravane mobile et l'architecture mexicaine. Un mirador prolongé d'un mur en stuc bleu achemine les visiteurs vers une immense porte en acier inoxydable. Cet accès débouche sur le vestibule où un escalier communique avec l'étage principal. S'inspirant de l'architecture populaire mexicaine, le rez-de-chaussée de la résidence est composé de murs chargés de textures et de couleurs. Le niveau inférieur abrite la chambre à coucher principale à une extrémité, un bureau à l'autre et une aire centrale occupée par la salle à manger, la cuisine et la bibliothèque. Le niveau supérieur, plus inspiré par la génération industrielle de logis mobiles, est un volume rectangulaire où le métal est roi.

Dieses Wohnhaus auf einem Hügel ist im Gegensatz zu oberflächlichen historischen Reproduktionen die Kombination zweier typischer, volkstümlicher Bauweisen der Region, nämlich eine Mischung aus dem beweglichen Mobilhome und der mexikanischen Architektur. Ein verlängerter Aussichtspunkt mit einer blau verputzten Mauer führt den Besucher zu einer ungewöhnlichen Tür aus rostigem Stahl. Diese Tür öffnet sich zu einer Diele, von der aus eine Treppe in den ersten Stock führt. Inspiriert von der volkstümlichen, mexikanischen Architektur besteht das Erdgeschoss des Hauses aus schweren Mauern mit grober und farbiger Oberfläche. Im Untergeschoss liegen auf einer Seite das große Schlafzimmer, auf der anderen Seite ein Büro und in der Mitte Speisezimmer, Küche und Bibliothek. Das obere Geschoss ist eher von der industriellen Generation der Mobilhomes inspiriert. Es handelt sich um einen rechteckigen Raum, indem als Material Metall dominiert.

Wide openings on to the hill and valley allow the breeze to penetrate the house and offer gratifying views of the mountainous landscape.

D'amples ouvertures orientées vers la colline et la vallée permettent à la brise de pénétrer la maison et offrent une superbe vue sur le paysage montagneux.

Weite Öffnungen zum Hügel und zum Tal dienen der Belüftung und bieten einen wundervollen Blick über die Berglandschaft.

The rear of the house is a relaxation area enhanced by trees and magnificent views.

Etant donné l'environnement arboré, la zone arrière a été aménagée pour le repos et la relaxation.

Der hintere Bereich, der zwischen Bäumen liegt und von dem aus man einen wunderschönen Ausblick hat, dient als Ruhe- und Entspannungszone.

Apartment in Borneo Eiland
Appartement à Bornéo-Eiland
Appartement in Borneo-Eiland

Amsterdam, Netherlands

Despite the strict building restrictions in force in Holland, the architects managed to construct a housing complex characterized by the uniqueness of each of the homes. The complex consists of three-story houses whose back patios face each other. In order to camouflage the sight of cars parked in rows, the architects inverted the section and created an inner street in which the parking lots are hidden by balconies. The inevitable concrete tunnel generated by the sequence of homes is softened by modifications to the design of the end houses in each row, whose big balconies jut out from the façades. To enhance the uniqueness of these buildings, different-colored translucent glass was used in each case.

Malgré les fortes restrictions d'urbanisme en vigueur dans ce pays, les architectes sont parvenus à ériger un complexe résidentiel défini par l'unicité de chacune des habitations. L'ensemble est constitué de maisons à trois étages dont les patios arrière se projettent l'un face à l'autre. Pour éviter l'image de voitures garées en enfilade, les architectes ont inversé la coupe pour créer une rue intérieure où les aires de garage sont masquées par les balcons. L'incontournable tunnel de béton de la structure, généré par l'enfilade de maisons, semble atténué grâce à une modification dans la conception des dernières habitations de chaque rangée, dotées de grands balcons qui dépassent de la façade. L'emploi de verre translucide de différentes couleurs, souligne la singularité de ces constructions.

Obwohl in diesem Land sehr strenge Bauvorschriften gelten, gelang es den Architekten, ein Wohngebäude zu errichten, das durch den einzigartigen Charakter jeder einzelnen Wohnung gekennzeichnet ist. Die Gruppe besteht aus dreistöckigen Häusern, deren Hinterhöfe einander gegenüber liegen. Um den Anblick einer Reihe geparkter Autos zu vermeiden, drehten die Architekten die normale Verteilung um und schufen eine innere Straße, auf der die Parkplätze von den Balkonen verborgen werden. Der unvermeidliche Betontunnel, der durch die aufeinanderfolgenden Wohnungen entsteht, wurde kaschiert, in dem die letzten Häuser der Reihe mit einem großen Balkon versehen wurden, der aus der Fassade herausragt. Um die Einzigartigkeit jedes Hauses zu unterstreichen, wurde lichtdurchlässiges Glas in verschiedenen Farben eingesetzt.

The attic differs from the other floors: the four rooms in the original plan have become a bright, open space.

L'attique de l'édifice est une variante par rapport aux autres étages. Les quatre chambres du plan original forment un espace diaphane.

Die Dachwohnung des Gebäudes ist anders als die anderen Wohnungen. Hier ist aus den vier Zimmern der Originalgrundrisse ein einziger, transparenter Raum geworden.

› Ground floor Rez-de-chaussée Erdgeschoss

› First floor Premier étage Erstes Obergeschoss

A central space contains all the services and installations, thereby conditioning the position of the different rooms.

Un espace central, contenant tous les services et installations, détermine la distribution des différentes pièces.

In einem zentralen Raum sind alle funktionellen Installationen untergebracht, was die Anordnung der verschiedenen Zimmer beeinflusst.

349

Vienna, Austria

Ray 1

The location of Ray 1, on the top floor of an office building dating from the 1960s, served as the starting point for the development of the project. The design, which inevitably had to comply with strict building regulations, shuns all manner of conventionalism: it was decided to adopt a steel framework that made it possible to evenly distribute the loads on the walls. The main thrusts are absorbed by the gable end while the remaining metallic elements serve to frame a glass wrapper. The result is one of astonishing lightness, an object that stands out magnificently against its urban surroundings. The form of the structure itself, as well as its permanent relationship with the immediate landscape, creates a dynamic environment inside and an opportunity to experience the exterior through terraces and large openings.

L'implantation de Ray 1, au dernier étage d'un édifice de bureaux datant des années soixante, sert de base de référence au développement du projet. Le design, respecte les normes d'urbanisme strictes et incontournables, sans tomber dans les clichés : le choix s'est porté sur une ossature d'acier qui permet de répartir régulièrement les charges sur les murs. Les charges principales reposent sur le pignon, tandis que les autres éléments métalliques servent de cadre à une chrysalide de verre. L'ensemble est ainsi paré d'une légèreté surprenante, formant un objet très intéressant dans le contexte urbain. La forme même de la structure, ainsi que la relation permanente avec le paysage environnant, imprime l'atmosphère intérieure de dynamisme et permet de capter l'extérieur au travers de terrasses et de grandes ouvertures.

Der Standort von Ray 1, das letzte Stockwerk eines Bürogebäudes aus den Siebzigerjahren, dient als Referenzpunkt für die Gesamtplanung. Bei der Gestaltung musste man die strengen Bauvorschriften beachten. Ein Stahlskelett verteilt die Lasten gleichmäßig auf die Mauern. Die Hauptlasten werden von der Seitenwand getragen, während die übrigen Elemente aus Metall als Rahmen für die Hülle aus Glas dienen. Das Ergebnis wirkt überraschend leicht und es entstand ein Objekt, das in seiner unmittelbaren Umgebung sehr interessant wirkt. Die Form der Struktur selbst und die ständige Beziehung zu der umgebenden Landschaft schaffen eine dynamische Atmosphäre im Inneren und die Möglichkeit, mit der äußeren Umgebung mithilfe von Terrassen und großen Öffnungen zu experimentieren.

The design of the large fourth-floor terrace had to comply with the strict building regulations in force.

Le design de la grande terrasse, située au quatrième étage, devait se conformer strictement aux normes d'urbanisme en vigueur.

Bei der Gestaltung der großen Terrasse im vierten Stock musste man sich an die strengen Bauvorschriften halten.

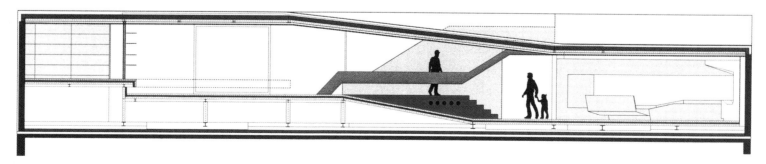

› Section Section Schnitt

The form of the structure, together with its permanent relationship with the surrounding landscape, creates a dynamic interior environment.

La forme même de la structure, ainsi que la relation constante avec le paysage environnant, imprime l'intérieur d'une atmosphère dynamique.

Die Form der Struktur selbst und die ständige Beziehung zur umgebenden Landschaft schaffen eine dynamische Atmosphäre im Inneren.

The sloping bedroom window accentuates the oblique slant of the bed head.

L'inclinaison de la fenêtre de la chambre accentue le caractère oblique du chevet du lit.

Die Neigung des Fensters im Schlafzimmer unterstreicht die Neigung des Kopfteils am Bett.

Apartment in San Francisco
Appartement à San Francisco
Appartement in San Francisco

San Francisco, USA

This apartment, the property of a photographer, is the extension of an existing industrial building. The owner wanted to convert this former factory into a studio. After a time, he thought he might exploit the advantages of its location to transform part of the structure into a home. The original building consisted of a rectangular basic unit with a timber beam ceiling. The new apartment, superimposed on the original structure, enjoys splendid views of the city and the bay. The apartment was designed as part of a series of successive spaces. While the floor below contains the studio, the floor above the apartment stretches out as if on a mezzanine and takes full advantage of the terrace. In this way, the domestic space is flooded with natural light while the studio is darker and more enclosed.

Cet appartement, appartenant à un photographe, est l'agrandissement d'un édifice industriel déjà existant. Le propriétaire voulait réhabiliter cette ancienne usine pour en faire son studio de photo. Au bout d'un certain temps, il a pensé optimiser les avantages offerts par le lieu pour transformer une partie de la structure en habitation. L'édifice original, une unité basique rectangulaire, était clos par une toiture en poutres de bois. La nouvelle habitation, superposée à la structure originale, bénéficie des splendides vues sur la ville et sur la baie. L'appartement a été conçu comme partie intégrante d'une série d'espaces successifs. Le studio est situé au niveau principal, tandis qu'à l'étage supérieur, l'habitation s'étend sous forme de mansarde et tire parti de la terrasse. De cette façon, les parties domestiques bénéficient au maximum de la lumière naturelle alors que le studio de photo, moins éclairé, est en retrait.

Dieses Appartement im Besitz eines Fotografen entstand durch die Erweiterung eines bereits existierenden Industriegebäudes. Der Eigentümer baute diese ehemalige Fabrik in ein Fotografiestudio um. Später kam er auf die Idee, diesen günstigen Standort zu nutzen, um einen Teil der Baustruktur in eine Wohnung umzugestalten. Das Originalgebäude besteht aus einer rechteckigen Basiseinheit, die von einem Dach mit Holzbalken gedeckt ist. Die neue Wohnung liegt über der Originalstruktur und man hat einen wundervollen Blick auf die Stadt und auf die Bucht. Das Appartement wurde als eine Art Abfolge verschiedener Räume entworfen. Das Studio befindet sich im Erdgeschoss, und im Obergeschoss liegt die Wohnung wie eine Art Zwischengeschoss. Die Terrasse verschönert das Gesamtbild. In alle Wohnbereiche fällt reichlich Tageslicht ein, während das Fotografiestudio dunkler und geschlossener ist.

The domestic space, located on the top floor of the building, takes maximum advantage of the natural light that filters through from the terrace.

Les parties domestiques, situées tout en haut de l'édifice, bénéficient au maximum de la lumière naturelle filtrée par la terrasse.

Die Wohnbereiche befinden sich im oberen Teil des Gebäudes. So wird das Licht ausgenutzt, das über die Terrasse einfällt.

The kitchen and the bathroom still maintain some of the elements of the original building, such as the timber beams that support part of the structure.

La cuisine et la salle de bains ont conservé certains aspects de l'édifice initial, comme les poutres de bois qui soutiennent une partie de la structure.

In der Küche und im Bad hat man einige Elemente des Originalgebäudes sowie die Holzbalken der Struktur erhalten.

Penthouse in São Paulo
Attique à São Paulo
Dachwohnung in São Paulo

São Paulo, Brazil

In his work, Arthur de Mattos Casas embraces many disciplines, to the point where it is hard to determine just how far his creativity goes. Like a Renaissance man - artist, architect, craftsman, and philosopher, a veritable hunter of concepts - this multi-faceted Brazilian works to establish a solid, coherent relationship between space and the objects that occupy it. On the one hand, the site, and on the other the utensils that serve to meet its needs, in both functional and perceptive terms. The interior design process carried out in this and other projects is marked by the contrast between the purity of rationalism and the sumptuousness of decoration. While rationalism champions formal essence vis-à-vis ornament, this apartment is clear evidence that both may exist side by side: the merit lies in their unification within a single concept and the design of objects that leave room for a degree of poetic license in the details.

Le travail d'Arthur de Mattos Casas embrassant de multiples disciplines, il n'est pas facile d'évaluer l'influence de sa créativité. A l'instar d'un homme de la Renaissance -artiste, architecte, artisan et philosophe chasseur de concepts- ce brésilien, aux multiples facettes, travaille pour créer une relation intense et harmonieuse entre l'espace et les objets qui l'intéressent. D'un côté, le lieu, et de l'autre, les ustensiles dont il a besoin, tant à l'échelle fonctionnelle que perceptive. Le processus de design intérieur réalisé dans ce projet et dans d'autres se distingue par l'opposition entre pureté du rationalisme et opulence de la décoration. Le rationalisme défend l'essence formelle face au décor. Cet appartement est la preuve que les deux tendances peuvent cohabiter, le mérite étant de les avoir unies pour créer un seul concept : créer des objets dont l'essence même permet une certaine liberté poétique dans la réalisation de détails.

Die Arbeit von Arthur de Mattos Casas erstreckt sich auf so viele verschiedene Disziplinen, dass es schwer zu sagen ist, bis wohin sich seine Kreativität auswirkt. Der Brasilianer arbeitete daran, eine starke Beziehung zwischen dem Raum und den darin enthaltenen Objekten zu schaffen. Einerseits ist da der Raum, andererseits gibt es die Elemente, die den Notwendigkeiten des Raumes dienen, sowohl auf funktioneller Ebene als auch in der Wahrnehmung. Bei der Innengestaltung dieser und anderer Räume existiert eine Gegenüberstellung der Reinheit des Rationalismus und der Üppigkeit der Dekoration. Der Rationalismus verteidigt die formelle Essenz gegen die Verzierungen. Diese Wohnung ist ein Beweis dafür, dass beide Tendenzen sich den gleichen Raum teilen können, indem man sie in einem einzigen Konzept vereint. Es wurden Objekte geschaffen, deren Essenz gewisse poetische Zugeständnisse in den Details zulässt.

The wooden stairway links the apartment's different levels.

L'escalier de bois relie les différents niveaux de l'habitation.

Die Holztreppe verbindet die verschiedenen Ebenen der Wohnung.

The use of the same materials throughout the apartment enhances the visual continuity between the public and private spaces.

L'emploi des mêmes matériaux dans tout l'appartement montre la continuité visuelle qui existe entre la sphère publique et la sphère privée.

Durch den Einsatz der gleichen Materialien in der gesamten Wohnung entstand eine visuelle Kontinuität zwischen den von allen benutzen Räumen und privateren Bereichen.

Magarola House
Maison Magarola
Haus Magarola

Barcelona, Spain

The transformation of this old building into an apartment complex forms part of the recent restoration process of the city. The materials and colors were chosen to create an environment with its own personality. The colors of the original beams having been taken as the point of reference, Iroko-wood furniture was chosen to contrast with the burnished stainless steel structures. The shelves and stairways, also of stainless steel, were conceived as elements superimposed on the furniture. The sofas and long curtains are in black, while red highlights some of the decorative elements, such as the Moroccan rug, the vase, and the artworks. The lamps were chosen not only for their design but also because they make it possible to regulate the intensity of the light according to the owner's tastes.

La transformation de cet ancien édifice en un complexe d'appartements fait partie des dernières réhabilitations effectuées dans cette ville. Les matériaux et les couleurs ont été choisis pour obtenir une atmosphère unique. Utilisant les couleurs des poutres d'origine comme point de référence, le choix s'est porté sur un mobilier de bois d'iroko contrastant avec les structures peaufinées de l'acier inoxydable. Les étagères et les escaliers, également en acier inoxydable, ont été conçus comme des éléments qui se superposent au mobilier. Le noir a été choisi pour le tissu des divans et des longs rideaux, le rouge pour accentuer certains éléments décoratifs, à l'instar du tapis marocain, de la jarre et des œuvres d'art. Les lampes ont été sélectionnées pour leur design mais aussi parce qu'elles permettent de régler l'intensité de la lumière selon les goûts du propriétaire.

Die Umgestaltung dieses alten Gebäudes in eine Reihe von Appartements ist ein Teil der letzten Renovierungen, die in dieser Stadt stattgefunden haben. Die Materialien und Farben wurden so ausgewählt, dass eine eigene Atmosphäre entstand. Die Farben der Originalbalken dienten als Ausgangspunkt. So wählte man Möbel aus Iroko, die zu den reinen Strukturen aus Edelstahl im Gegensatz stehen. Die Geländer und die Treppen sind ebenfalls aus Edelstahl und dienen als Elemente, die das Mobiliar beherrschen. Die Sofas und die langen Gardinen sind schwarz, und einige Dekorationselemente wie der marokkanischen Teppich, der Krug und die Kunstwerke werden von der Farbe Rot unterstrichen. Die Lampen wählte man nicht nur aufgrund ihres Designs aus, man kann mit ihnen auch die Intensität des Lichtes nach Wunsch zu verändern.

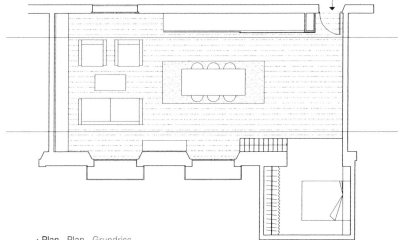

› Plan Plan Grundriss

› Bathroom plan Plan du bain Badezimmerplan

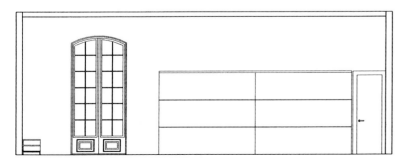

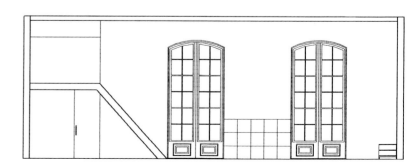

› Sections Sections Schnitte

Union Square Loft

Loft Union Square

Loft Union Square

New York, USA

One of the intentions of the architects before embarking on the transformation of this space was to go against its irregular geometry in order to enhance the magnificent views of the city. The restrained but by no means minimalist decor is based on the use of symmetry and neutral colors to create a homogeneous, versatile space. The distribution of the loft is articulated around a central nucleus consisting of the kitchen and the bathroom, and it offers uninterrupted views through the windows. The criteria governing the design were to seek functional solutions that facilitate habitability and give priority to multipurpose elements. One of the solutions was to allow the small reading area behind the living room to be turned into a guest bedroom as required by pushing the sliding panels down into the floor to set up the convertible bed hidden in the wall.

Avant d'initier la réhabilitation de cet espace, les architectes ont proposé, entre autres, d'aller à l'encontre de la géométrie irrégulière du plan pour profiter des magnifiques vues sur la ville. La décoration est sobre, sans être minimaliste, cherchant à employer la symétrie et les couleurs neutres pour créer un espace harmonieux et polyvalent. L'univers spatial est organisé autour d'un noyau central constitué de la cuisine et de la salle de bains, pour favoriser les vues panoramiques de l'extérieur au travers des fenêtres. La conception, en quête de solutions qui facilitent la vie des propriétaires au sein de leur habitat, s'est concentrée sur des éléments pluri fonctionnels. Une des solutions consiste à tirer parti de l'espace de lecture réduit derrière le salon pour le transformer en chambre d'amis en poussant les panneaux coulissants vers le sol pour installer le lit convertible, encastré dans le mur.

Eines der Ziele des Architekten vor dem Umbau war es, die unregelmäßige Geometrie des Grundrisses zu beheben, um den wundervollen Blick auf die Stadt besser zu nutzen. Die Dekoration ist schlicht, jedoch nicht minimalistisch. Gesucht wurde die Symmetrie und durch neutrale Farben entstand ein einheitlicher und vielseitiger Raum. Der Raum verteilt sich um einen zentralen Kern, der aus der Küche und dem Bad besteht. Man hat durch die Fenster einen freien Blick nach draußen. Man suchte nach funktionellen Lösungen, die die Wohnung für die Eigentümer komfortabel machen. Dazu wurden multifunktionelle Elemente geschaffen. Eine dieser Lösungen bestand darin, dass man den kleinen Leseraum hinter dem Wohnzimmer in ein Gästezimmer verwandeln kann, in dem man die Schiebepaneele in den Boden drückt, um ein Klappbett aufzustellen, das in der Wand versteckt ist.

The space was reconverted and opened to the exterior to frame the views of the city in the windows.

L'espace a été reconverti et ouvert vers l'extérieur pour encadrer les vues de la ville grâce au périmètre de fenêtres.

Der Raum wurde umgestaltet und nach außen geöffnet, um den wundervollen Blick über die Stadt freizugeben.

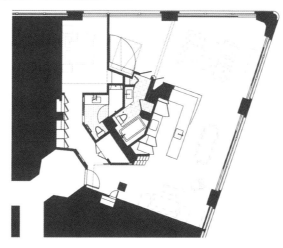

› Plan   Plan   Grundriss

The kitchen, dining room, and living room share the same open, all-encompassing space, organized around the layout of the elements.

La cuisine, la salle à manger et le salon se lovent au sein du même espace ouvert, organisé par la distribution des éléments.

Die Küche, das Speisezimmer und das Wohnzimmer befinden sich im gleichen offenen Raum, der durch die Verteilung der Elemente selbst organisiert wird.

Photo Credits Crédits photographiques Fotonachweis